"*THE BREAKAWAY BRAND* is a breakaway book… a must-read if you're a believer in brands and strategic marketing. The authors know their subject matter and bring new insights and 'to do's' to every serious marketer and member of senior management. The case studies here are extremely relevant and well articulated. Don't tread water—make a splash with your brands!"

—*Peter Klein*, SVP, Strategy and
Business Development, The Gillette Company

"In today's fast-paced world of media overload, *THE BREAKAWAY BRAND* highlights fundamental principles that enable marketers to protect and build their most valuable brand assets. The authors have developed some simple but powerful techniques aimed at breaking through the clutter and focusing marketing dollars in ways that give your brand a chance to win. This book will help CEOs and CMOs deliver maximum impact for their marketing dollar to sustain and grow high-impact brands."

—*Stephen Pagliuca*, Managing Director, Bain Capital

"The most compelling point in the book is that breakaway brands start with a deep commitment from the top. It is the CEO, COO, or CMO who act as the brand visionary; every 'Chief Officer' must be passionate, brave, and relentless. That's why this is a must read for every 'Chief.'"

—*Ken Romanzi*, Chief Operating
Officer-Domestic, Ocean Spray Cranberries

"Building highly effective marketing campaigns is a complex challenge. *THE BREAKAWAY BRAND* is a valuable read for anyone committed to taking their marketing game to the next level."

—*John Quelch*, Senior Associate Dean and Lincoln Filene
Professor of Business Administration, Harvard Business School

"Breaking away *and staying ahead* is what this book is all about! This is a truly unusual look 'inside' at what it takes to be and remain great by many of the best in business today. I'm humbled and inspired."

—*Jeffrey J. Jones II*, EVP, Global Marketing, Gap, Inc.

"*THE BREAKAWAY BRAND* is a fun read and a real deep-dive into the many ways breakaway brands have risen to the top. Clearly, the authors understand the mechanics of getting brands to operate at optimum potential."

—*Lee Ann Daly*, EVP, Marketing, ESPN, Inc.

"*THE BREAKAWAY BRAND* is much more than an essential study of marketing and branding. This is a demonstration of the necessity of passion, integrity, quality, and leadership in business. The authors have drawn important life lessons for all of us from a detailed study of one key facet of business."

—*Wycliffe Grousbeck*, Principal Owner, Boston Celtics

"The authors take an extraordinarily complex marketing issue and break it down into something simple you can apply to your business. *THE BREAKAWAY BRAND* is refreshingly no BS; I can't imagine you won't be smarter for having read it."

—*David Lubars*, Chairman and
Chief Creative Officer, BBDO North America

"The authors have masterfully created a case-study driven, clearly articulated tutorial on the why's and how's of successful branding. *THE BREAKAWAY BRAND* is 'the bible' for anyone seeking success with brand names or branded products."

—*Ted W. Beneski*, Managing Partner & CEO, Insight Equity

"Building brands in today's complex, difficult marketing environment presents unique challenges and opportunities. *THE BREAKAWAY BRAND* shines a light on some of the best brands in the world and reveals how they sustain success. The principles that the authors uncover will make any brand marketer better."

—*Kevin L. Keller*, E.B. Osborn Professor
of Marketing, Tuck School of Business

"At a time when marketers are increasingly questioning the value of advertising, *THE BREAKAWAY BRAND* presents a number of recent and highly relevant campaigns that demonstrate what can happen when advertising fires on all cylinders."

—*Bob Pagano*, Partner, Monitor Group

"With brands as in life, everyone wants to go to heaven, but no one wants to die: absent wisdom, powerful creativity can seem terrifying. *THE BREAKAWAY BRAND* demolishes risk with expertise and supplants fear with inspiration. Heaven on earth is possible—at least for your brand."

—*Jim Mullen*, Founder, Mullen Advertising

"The authors remind us that every product and service, even commodity products like popcorn and vodka, can become 'breakaway brands.' These days when so much effort goes into lowering costs, and it seems that everything is going offshore, the authors show us how to take responsibility for something that can never be outsourced: Building your brand!"

—*Alan Botsford*, Partner, Parthenon Capital

THE
BREAKAWAY BRAND

HOW GREAT BRANDS STAND OUT

Francis J. Kelly III
Barry Silverstein

McGraw-Hill

New York   Chicago   San Francisco
Lisbon   London   Madrid   Mexico City
Milan   New Delhi   San Juan
Seoul   Singapore   Sydney   Toronto

The Breakaway Brand: How Great Brands Stand Out

1234567890 DOC DOC 0198765

ISBN 0-07-226237-0

The sponsoring editor for this book was Marjorie McAneny and the project editor was LeeAnn Pickrell. The copy editor was Emily Wolman, the proofreader was Susie Elkind, and the indexer was Karin Arrigoni. Composition and illustration by ITC. Cover design by Jeff Weeks.

This book was composed with Adobe® InDesign®.

Library of Congress Cataloging-in-Publication Data

Kelly, Francis J., 1956-
    The breakaway brand: how great brands stand out / by Francis J. Kelly, III and Barry Silverstein.
        p. cm.
    ISBN 0-07-226237-0
    1. Brand name products--Marketing. I. Silverstein, Barry,
1948- II. Title.
    HD69.B7K455 2005
    658.8'27--dc22
                                        2005015991

CONTENTS

ACKNOWLEDGMENTS

Building a breakaway brand comes from a deep understanding of the consumer. This rare and special insight helps create truly exceptional brands that sustain success over a long period of time.

In writing this book, we looked at some of the best marketing in the world executed on behalf of such brands. We were impressed by the work we evaluated. We wanted to test our own agency's work against these high standards. We were fortunate to realize that many of our clients are deserving of breakaway brand status.

We dedicate this book to all those who build breakaway brands. People outside our agency like Alex Bogusky, David Lubars, Steve Jobs, and Lou Gerstner inspired us. People inside Arnold Worldwide inspired us as well—our CEO Ed Eskandarian, our Chairman and Chief Creative Officer Ron Lawner, the Arnold Board, Karen Driscoll, Pete Favat, John Staffen, and hundreds of others at our agency who help build award-winning programs for our clients.

We are fortunate and grateful to work with many outstanding clients. In this book, we reference Acushnet (FootJoy and Titleist), American Legacy Foundation (truth), Brown-Forman (Jack Daniel's), Citizens Bank, Royal Caribbean, Tyson, Volkswagen, and Vonage. We would also like to acknowledge every marketing person at all of the client organizations we serve. You are the folks who make our working relationship so rewarding.

We would especially like to thank Larry Fish and Theresa McLaughlin of Citizens Bank, Adam Goldstein of Royal Caribbean International, and Dan Hanrahan of Celebrity Cruises for taking the time to share their stories, and Ron Lawner for sharing his creative insights.

For their valuable input and advice, we thank Jeff Hicks, Peter Klein, David Lubars, Jim Mullen, Bob Pagano, Steve Pagliuca, and Steve Wilhite.

Thanks to Bill Alberti at Arnold for his analytical expertise. These additional folks at Arnold played a role in helping us make this book a reality: Margaret Ahnell, Cara Banisch, Will Burns, Caryl Capeci, Lois Casaubon, Paul Charbonnier, Lenora Cushing, Sarah Fleischman, Mary Francioso, Nicole Harvey, Brent Harwood, Jaime Hrubala, Anne Joynt, Tina Klaric, Don Lane, Heather Lewis, Patty Limjap, Ryan McLaughlin, Lisa Mercier, Paul Nelson, Chuck Nussmeyer, Susan Ogren, Neela Pal, Barb Reilly, Phil Reilly, John Raftery, Joe Roman, Andrew Rosenzweig, Kelly Schrader, Melanie Seaborn, Michael Stuart, Marilyn Turner, Meredith Vellines, Lily Weitzman, Amy Wilcox, and Ron Wilcox. Thanks to Charlisse Chang, an Arnold intern who helped compile information about the brands cited in this book. There are many others at Arnold who touched this book in some way. Our apologies that we could not mention everyone.

For their contributions, we thank Kristina Hagbard, ABSOLUT; Dave Verklin, Carat Americas; Paul Rogers and Robin Uhl, *Chief Executive* magazine; Katherine Stone, Decent Marketing; Jordan Berman, Showtime; Anne Saunders, Starbucks; John Beystehner, UPS; Stuart Karp, Volkswagen; and Kelly Miano, White Wave.

We thank our publisher, McGraw-Hill: Jeffrey Krames for his belief in this book, Margie McAneny for her editorial guidance, and the fine editors and staff who helped produce a breakaway book.

Finally, a heartfelt thanks to our families who manage to always smile and support us—no matter how many hours we devote to this crazy business.

—*Fran Kelly and Barry Silverstein*

INTRODUCTION

Each year in the United States alone, companies invest nearly $300 billion marketing their goods and services. A considerable portion of this investment is spent promoting thousands of new branded products that enter the marketplace. Most of these new products fail. In fact, few brands succeed in separating themselves from the rest.

With so much money at stake, we need to ask why only a small number of brands successfully break away from the competition.

I don't believe the success of these brands can be attributed to the size of their advertising budgets, or the luxury of having the best-known brand names. For example, Altoids mints were introduced in the U.S. with a tiny ad budget and at a product price that was three times its nearest competitor, yet Altoids became the number one brand in its category. JetBlue was a new, unknown airline brand, yet it was profitable in its first year of operation. It achieved the highest operating margin of any domestic U.S. airline just two years after its launch, while four out of five competing airlines were either in bankruptcy or close to it.

Brands like Altoids and JetBlue are what the authors of this book refer to as "breakaway brands." These brands, along with brands such as ABSOLUT, Apple, Nike, and Volkswagen, are part of a small but select group that has found a way to survive and thrive in an over-crowded marketplace.

I believe there are three key reasons brands such as these succeed against all odds:

- First, most breakaway brands base their success on *unique characteristics*. These characteristics may include superior performance or another unique product benefit, unique positioning, a unique physical environment, unique packaging, or unique distribution. Whatever the specific characteristic, a breakaway brand must create a clear and distinct separation from its competitors. That separation can be proven—because it can be measured by the sales of the product, the market share, or the brand value.

- Second, advertising can significantly contribute to the success of a breakaway brand and on occasion, advertising can in and of itself *create* a breakaway brand. Take the famous "got milk?" campaign as an example. This was the beginning of a breakaway campaign that changed the American public's perception of milk. Before this campaign, every ad about milk conveyed how good it was for you and how it built strong bones. "got milk?" changed everything because it recognized not the typical health benefits, but rather the contemporary place of milk in the American diet. Milk became relevant again, because it was the perfect companion beverage to junk food like peanut butter and cookies and chocolate cake. And, as an aside, it was good for you. The "got milk?" campaign broke milk away from its previous image and as a result, milk became a breakaway beverage.

- Third, behind every breakaway brand is a *team* working toward a common goal—and a *champion* leading the team. Typically, you'll find that the team is comprised of internal marketing staff at the brand marketer, along with numerous people from the marketer's ad agency. It is the close working partnership between the marketer and agency—the respect they have for each other, the relationship they share, the passion they have for the brand—that creates the "magic." Furthermore, great breakaway brands succeed year after year because of a brand champion at the top. This may be the CEO or the President, the CMO, or some combination of top executives. But it is rare for a breakaway brand to succeed without the commitment of senior management at the highest levels of an organization.

Becoming a breakaway brand is not a simple proposition, especially in light of a dramatically changing marketplace. There is more competition among brands, but there is also more competition among media channels. It is becoming harder and harder for advertisers to get consumers to notice a brand, much less make an informed purchase decision.

The fact is that too many brands are simply copying others instead of being unique. Not enough brands stand out. Not enough brands amaze and delight customers. The message of this book is that we cannot let our brands become commodities. We must create brands with a difference, and we must find ways to make these brands stand out.

Successful brands are not just great marketing stories—they are great business stories. What a breakaway brand can do for a company is not insignificant. A breakaway brand enables a company to raise prices and decrease incentive expenses, because the strength of the brand allows it to be sold at a premium price. A breakaway brand helps a company weather economic downturns and even product problems or company controversy, because consumers are forgiving about brands they love. On the financial side, a breakaway brand can be proven to lead to rising stock price PE ratios and increased company valuation.

The importance of this book, therefore, reaches beyond the advertising and marketing world alone. The authors address what a brand must do to break away in packaging, advertising, on the Internet, and in other areas one would traditionally think of as marketing. However, they also discuss the need for product innovation, highlight the importance of support from chief executives, and demonstrate how breakaway brands produce proven results.

I'm privileged to have partnered with senior executives from some of America's true breakaway brands during more than 30 years in the advertising business. I can tell you that the impact a breakaway brand has on consumers' lives is a significant measure of the brand's success—but the impact the brand has on its company's shareholders can be equally significant.

—*Ed Eskandarian*
Chief Executive Officer
Arnold Worldwide

CHAPTER 1

Breaking Away from the Sea of Gray

W hy don't more brands break away?
Why are the majority of brands "me-too," look-alike products?

Why aren't more brands like Nike in athletic wear, Apple in computers and consumer electronics, BMW and Volkswagen in autos, Altoids in confections, Budweiser in beer, JetBlue in airlines, Royal Caribbean in cruises?

Why don't more brands invest in memorable advertising campaigns, smartly integrated media, and strategic plans that last for more than five years?

Why don't more CEOs *demand* that their brands break away?

Why is the passion gone? What happened to the "joy in branding," as Ron Lawner, Chairman and Chief Creative Officer of Arnold Worldwide, puts it. "It's heartbreaking how many brands don't get their due," says Lawner. "I think of brand advertising as an art, but I haven't found a lot of art lovers in corporate America."

One of the reasons why brands don't break away is that many corporations are driven by fear and the bottom line. Not enough heads of marketing are willing to take the risk it requires to do great work, and not enough CEOs know what great work is, according to Lawner.

Advertising that doesn't stand out isn't the only problem. Brands are flooding the marketplace—yet consumers can't distinguish one from another. The number of new packaged goods introduced from 1990 to 2000 rose almost 100 percent, from nearly 16,000 to nearly 32,000. From 1999 to 2000, the number of such introductions increased over 20 percent, the largest single year increase in the past decade.[1] Nearly 27,000 new household and food products were introduced in 2003 alone.[2]

And that's only packaged goods. It doesn't include other types of products, or branded services in travel, entertainment, telecommunications, and financial services.

Every day, we are bombarded with thousands of messages about such brands. Of every 60 minutes on prime time TV, about 17 minutes are commercials. Brand advertising and promotion surrounds us and colors our world. It is there when we flip through a magazine, when we listen to the radio in the car, when we walk down a city street, when we sit at our computers. Messages about brands penetrate our thoughts and, marketers hope, influence our buying decisions.

This brand overload is too much for consumers to handle. With so many brands to consider, and so many messages to process, consumers glaze over. Nothing gets through, nothing stands out. Brands are lost in an indistinguishable sea of gray.

Every once in a while, a memorable brand briefly bobs to the surface, only to be swallowed up by the waves again. The consumer gets a glimpse of the brand before it submerges into the sea of gray.

There are brands that everyone recognizes, brands that stand out in the crowd, and others that live in their shadows. Nike outshines Reebok. Titleist golf balls outshine Top Flite. IBM outshines HP. Why is that? How does that happen?

It isn't easy. Companies that make products, and agencies that promote them, perpetuate a lack of brand differentiation. Kevin Clancy and Jack Trout observed in "Brand Confusion" (*Harvard Business Review,* March 2002) that, of 46 major product categories, consumers thought brands were converging, or becoming less distinct, in 40 of them. Clancy and Trout concluded: "With the proliferation of new brands and endless brand extensions, more and more categories seem to be sliding toward commodity status.... Without a clear differentiating idea attached to a brand, all you're left with to motivate buyers is price."

We don't believe it has to be this way. Products can stand out. Brands *can* break away. Consumers want the next new thing. To be different is to be great. But it takes hard work, guts, and creativity. And sometimes it takes the ability to make tough sacrifices and maybe even risk everything.

That's what this book is about. It's about the brand that stands out, not just in its own product category, but from all other brands. It's about the brand that achieves huge results. It's about the brand that breaks away. And it's about the why and how of building a breakaway brand.

In this book, we'll look at what it takes to become a breakaway brand: what it really means, how a brand can break away, and how today's great brands execute breakaway campaigns, packaging, and promotion. We'll look at how the Internet has become a breakaway agent, and how a CEO can become a breakaway hero. And finally, we'll discuss the outstanding results that breakaway brands are achieving, then leave you with some specific rules for building your own breakaway brand.

The New Marketing Reality

Only a handful of brands rise above commodity status. One reason is that very few marketing programs do anything to make brands break through the surface of the sea of gray. Fact is, a lot of promotional campaigns are just plain mediocre.

Only a handful of brands rise above commodity status. One reason is that very few marketing programs do anything to make brands break through the surface of the sea of gray.

There is a new marketing reality at work that makes it harder for brands to break through. It used to be that consumers were fairly easy to reach through "standard" media. Television influenced the masses, newspapers and magazines had healthy circulations and ad revenue, direct mail achieved respectable response rates, and e-mail was a newly emerging novelty.

All that has changed. This is the era of consumer choice and control. A TV commercial can be zapped by TiVo, telemarketing calls can be blocked by "Do Not Call" lists, printed newspapers are regarded as dinosaurs, direct mail gets tossed in the trash before it's opened, and e-mail can be stopped with antispam filters and Federal legislation.

Consumers are tuning out promotional messages that bombard them through these various channels. The level of brand saturation is so great that most of us naturally employ a screen-sort-discard process. So while marketers pay lip service to "relationship marketing" and "creating ongoing dialogues with consumers," the reality is that only a handful of brands have a lasting impact on audiences.

Brand proliferation is running rampant. Most brands follow rather than lead. Basic brand advertising is losing its effectiveness because nothing unique or compelling is presented to the consumer. That's why smart brand marketers must use a new arsenal of strategies and tactics. It is no longer good enough to create great brand advertising in a vacuum. There is a new sense of urgency around precisely targeted marketing to audience segments.

As a result, advertising is being redefined as a discipline with no boundaries. The media mix is changing. Network television advertising is no longer the accepted dominant medium for a core brand-awareness campaign. Cable television, with its narrowcasting capabilities, is an essential part of the mix. Online media (web sites, e-mail, search engine strategies, online advertising) play an increasingly important role in positioning and differentiating brands.

"Advertainment" (product placements in and sponsorships of television shows and movies) is a key tactic for increasing brand awareness. "Guerilla marketing" (special events, street teams, and seemingly random product promotion) should be built into most brand launches. Experiential marketing that creates personal involvement between the consumer and the product is in vogue. Nowadays marketing is all about how to blend together the right media to reach the right audience with the right message at the right time.

WHY MOST BRANDS DESERVE TO FAIL

Most new products fail—and they deserve to. Most products in a category look alike. Rather than risk being different or innovative, many products start and end their lives as me-too brands. They take the safe road and emulate the characteristics of the category leader. This actually enhances rather than displaces the leading brand's position, because it reinforces the attributes that made the leader a leader in the first place. Once a category-leading brand, or "first mover," establishes a dominating presence, it is hard for other brands to rise to the top.

Most new products fail, and they deserve to. Most products in a category look alike. Rather than risk being different or innovative, many products start and end their lives as me-too brands.

As Michael Porter notes in his book *Competitive Advantage: Creating and Sustaining Superior Performance* (Free Press, 1998), "It is striking how many firms that were first movers have remained leaders for decades. In consumer goods, for example, such leading brands as Crisco, Ivory, Life Savers, Coca-Cola, Campbell's, Wrigley, Kodak, Lipton, and Goodyear were leaders by the 1920s."

We have seen some evolution in category leadership as the consumer becomes a more discerning buyer. Today's consumer understands there can be more than one formidable brand in a category. Coke and Pepsi, McDonald's and Burger King, and Honda and Toyota are good examples of this.

Yet acceptance of additional brands in a category can make brand differentiation more difficult, and the result can be a reduction in brand preference. While the consumer might prefer Diet Coke, she may readily accept Diet Pepsi when her preferred choice isn't available. At some point, she may drink either one, interchangeably. That's a problem for all leading brands.

It is the continuing expansion of brand choice that creates a paradox—the reduction of the consumer's ability to make choices. In the introduction to his intriguing book *The Paradox of Choice: Why More Is Less* (Ecco, 2004), Barry Schwartz says: "...as the number of choices keeps growing, negative aspects of having a multitude of options begin to appear. As the number of choices grows further, the negatives escalate until we become overloaded. At this point, choice no longer liberates, but debilitates."

Categories are being flooded with look-alike products, and the result is that points of differentiation are lost. If all products are commodities, what is the benefit of choice?

MAKING THE CHOICE TO BREAK AWAY

If you own a brand, ask yourself: What if your brand were out of stock in a retail store? Would a consumer wait until your brand becomes available, travel to another store to buy it…or purchase another brand instead? This is a brand's moment of truth. It speaks to real brand differentiation and loyalty.

Product marketers with me-too brands and consumers who are overloaded with choices are partners in a symbiotic vicious circle. You might say they are both helping each other drown in a sea of gray.

What if your brand were out of stock in a retail store? Would a consumer wait until your brand becomes available, travel to another store to buy it...or purchase another brand instead? This is a brand's moment of truth.

The lack of choice is evident in many product categories. Take the U.S. cell phone market as an example. To date, no major provider has truly differentiated itself over another in this billion-dollar marketplace. The more providers attempt to break away, the more they look and sound the same.

Cell phone providers offer similar cell phone products, manufactured by the same vendors, with similar coverage via similar cellular networks. Cell phone providers are competing fiercely for the same customers, sometimes on the same turf. They're all me-too brands. That's why the churn rate—the percentage of customer turnover—is so high in this category.

Our company's Boston headquarters is located in an office building attached to one of the city's leading upscale shopping malls. In a heavy traffic area right near our building, two permanent booths are set up, literally opposite one other, representing two different cell phone providers. Walk a minute or two down a corridor, and you'll find two more cell phone providers with kiosks set up directly across from one another. All the promotions are for free phones or free minutes. The brands are virtually interchangeable.

Market conditions like these naturally lead to brand upheaval and industry consolidation. In December 2004, Sprint and Nextel announced they would merge. Earlier that year, Cingular announced it would acquire AT&T Wireless, leap-frogging the leader, Verizon Wireless, to create the largest U.S. wireless company. Lest you think this will reduce brand confusion, consider this: AT&T (the corporation, not AT&T Wireless itself) announced just months later that it would reintroduce wireless service by reselling another provider's offerings.

All this category confusion can actually provide an opportunity for a smart brand—a breakaway brand—to present a new choice to the marketplace. Virgin Mobile did just that, entering the category in July 2002. Virgin Mobile's approach was decid-edly different from everyone else's. The company targeted the untapped market of 15- to 24-year-olds with a prepaid plan rather than lengthy contracts. The brand relied on the awareness of Virgin and its brash and rebellious founder, Richard Branson, as its cachet, appealing to the antiauthority inclination of the youth market.

Virgin Mobile is supplementing an aggressive pricing strat-egy with edgy, sometimes outrageous advertising to break through the clutter and appeal to its target audience. Despite being outspent by its competitors on the order of 20 to 1, Virgin Mobile has acquired over 3 million customers in less than three years. Seventy percent of those customers are under age 30, and sixty percent are new to wireless, according to the company. By 2005, industry analysts acknowledged Virgin Mobile as a trendsetter brand, and it had become the number eight wireless carrier in the U.S.

Virgin Mobile took a lot of risks along the way. Some of the company's advertising might even be regarded as tasteless. But Virgin Mobile's mission was to offer a new choice, put a new spin on a product, and find a receptive audience. Even in the undifferentiated, crowded category of cellular phone providers, there is a way to break away.

A NEW DEFINITION OF THE 80/20 RULE

The Pareto principle, or 80/20 Rule, has long been a tenet of marketing. The principle addresses the relationship of customer or market segments, generally highlighting those that dominate others. It has been interpreted in a variety of ways, but one of the most popular definitions is this: *80 percent of a company's revenue comes from 20 percent of its customers.*

This principle is unwaveringly accurate for a majority of companies, regardless of their business type, size, or customer base. While the percentages may change, the relationship often proves to be true—that a small number of customers accounts for the bulk of the revenue.

We propose a new definition of the 80/20 Rule. It relates to the current condition of the brand world:

80 percent of brands are merely treading water in a sea of gray. Only 20 percent are making waves.

A deluge of undifferentiated brands is flooding the market. The majority of new brands fail. A fraction of category leaders become stronger and dominant. In order to succeed, some brands create new categories, possibly targeting smaller rather than larger consumer segments. The success or failure of these brands is now subject to the consumer's response, not the marketer's efforts. Consumer preference is an unforgiving force in the marketplace, weeding out and eliminating the weaker brands.

Here are four compelling reasons why only 20 percent or less of brands that exist today are breakaway brands.

1. BRANDS, LIKE THE COMPANIES THAT CREATE THEM, TYPICALLY RUN IN HERDS AND DON'T HAVE DISTINCTIVE VOICES. The natural inclination of brands is to move together and follow

a leader rather than differentiate themselves and break away from the pack. Marketers and their agencies find it difficult to fight category inertia. The road most traveled is adhering to the rules set by the brand category leader rather than promoting the brand in a new and different way. This also leads to *lack of a strong brand voice*: Brands talk about how great they are instead of about how they fit into the consumer's life. Some brands, in fact, are losing their relevance to consumers. A lack of differentiation, combined with a lack of relevance, is a death knell for a modern brand.

2. **COMPANIES ARE, FOR THE MOST PART, RISK-AVERSE.** While brand marketers may willingly invest in launching a product, it takes more than money alone to create a separate and distinctly different brand. Today, launching a brand or growing market share requires an aggressive and potentially risky brand–building and marketing strategy. Brand marketers tend to overtest to ensure success and end up with formulaic instead of breakaway marketing. Most companies won't take a chance on something that could backfire, possibly undermining profits and upsetting shareholders.

3. **BRANDS WON'T SUCCEED WITHOUT INTERNAL CHAMPIONS.** To be a breakaway brand, a brand must do many things right— and integrate all aspects of a marketing program flawlessly. This takes solid strategic thinking, a significant dollar investment, and support at the CEO and CMO level. A breakaway brand is unlikely to succeed without a strong team on the inside, a smart agency partner on the outside, and, ultimately, the backing of a CEO who is as marketing–savvy as he or she is financially adept. This just doesn't happen all that often.

4. **IT'S A COMPLETELY DIFFERENT MARKETING LANDSCAPE.** Thousands upon thousands of brands exist today, causing an ultracompetitive marketing environment. To even be noticed and heard, a brand must be distinctly different. Advertisers and their agencies are slowly waking up to this new reality, one in which old rules are gone and new rules are still being established. Most advertisers have not yet adjusted to the dramatic shift in consumer-driven marketing. Only some advertisers understand that the consumer now calls the shots and realize it's time to take greater risks and use breakaway strategies.

Look-alikes Are Everywhere

The look-alike, me-too product phenomenon is evident in category after category, as demonstrated in the following examples.

PITCHING LOW CARBS

Consider the "low carb" trend in foods. From 2000 to 2004, over 3,700 low-carb products were introduced. During the first half of 2004, such product introductions had tripled from the year before.[3] This trend was a case in which concern over obesity intersected with several popular diets (Atkins and South Beach, to name just two), creating a product subbrand category focused on a single characteristic: low carbohydrates. Once the trend gained traction, it seemed as if every food manufacturer joined in. No one wanted to risk being left behind. Low-carb subbranding has appeared on every type of food product, even cola. It has made its way into fast-food chains and restaurants, and has shown up on supplements in health food and drug stores.

While some marketers merely relabeled existing products that were already low in carbs, others did indeed produce new products in an effort to gain market share. The whole industry moved in a herd.

Industry experts say results have been mixed. ACNielsen reported that, while sales of low-carb foods rose almost 100 percent from fourth quarter 2003 to first quarter 2004, they then plummeted in the second quarter, growing at just over 40 percent. In the third quarter of 2004, they grew only about 6 percent. The low-carb beer category is a good example of products that failed.

These ups and downs may be indicative of a food fad that has run its course. The very nature of the low-carb diet created a fair amount of controversy, and in the meantime, the wary consumer did not necessarily buy into low-carb everything...especially when he discovered the higher price of low-carb brands. "Low carb" became simply another variation of undifferentiated brands in the sea of gray.

EXTENDING THE CHOICES IN CONSUMER PRODUCTS

Take a stroll down the toothpaste aisle in your local drug store and look for your favorite brand. You're likely to see a dizzying array of offerings that may occupy several shelves, ranging from "tartar protection" to "total protection" toothpaste, as well as gels, children's flavors, whitening products, and even toothbrushes—all under a particular brand name.

Search the laundry detergent, soap, soft drink, and cereal aisles in your grocery store and you'll see more of the same. These variations on a single brand name are called *brand extensions.*

Consumer products companies often extend the power of a brand name to another line of products in an effort to win market share. In theory, if consumers are provided with many choices having a familiar and trusted brand name, more products are likely to be sold. Just as important, the brand name begins to occupy more and more precious shelf space, making it difficult for competitors to be noticed.

You may have thought you were going to the store to make a simple purchasing decision—but it just isn't that easy today. Even if you're able to select a particular brand name (a difficult enough task in itself), choosing among all the products offered under that brand name is a challenge.

The brand extension strategy is pervasive in the marketing of consumer products. When two competing brands provide essentially the same brand extensions, the consumer may perceive all of them to be pretty much the same. As a result, real product choice may become trivialized.

Nonetheless, consumer products companies continue to use brand extension to grow their brands—and their market share. If it didn't work, they wouldn't do it. But brand extension makes one start to wonder: Is a shelf full of the same brand name, with seemingly endless product variations, simply too much for the consumer to absorb?

HOW DIFFERENT IS YOUR BANK?

Are there significant differences that made you choose your bank over another? Or did you choose your bank for the convenience of its branch or ATM locations? For the most part, the banking industry reinforces more similarities than differences. Checking and savings accounts, mortgages, home equity lines, credit and debit cards, branch hours, and ATM networks look pretty much the same, blending from bank to bank.

With an increasing number of bank mergers and acquisitions, though, it is more common than ever for consumers to see their bank brand name change. Ironically, only when your bank is acquired by another one might you start thinking about the differences between banks.

Suppose you have a relationship with a bank for a number of years, and another entity not well known to you acquires that bank. Your familiar, comfortable bank now has a new look, new account statements, new products, and maybe even new fees. Perhaps the tellers are the same when you walk into your branch, but everything else has changed.

When it comes to your hard-earned money, you probably don't respond well to change. In fact, you could easily experience some level of brand trauma at the loss of your old bank. You might resent the fact that a new bank from out of the area acquired your "local" bank—or you may fear that the service you now get will be less personal.

Most banks have not done a good job of differentiating themselves from their competitors. Many take their customers for granted, because they know customers are hesitant to move their accounts. But when your bank changes its brand, you may ask yourself if the "new" bank will serve your needs. You may be left with an uneasy feeling about the new bank, even if the services are basically the same as the old bank. Unless the newly named bank does something to reinforce its relationship with you as a customer, this is the time you might actually consider switching banks.

THE ME-TOO AIRLINES

While one could see how spiraling costs, September 11, and intense competition have created an untenable situation for airlines, it is also obvious that the major airline carriers have done little to differentiate themselves. The major carriers tend to move as a unit when they set prices, establish routes, add business class seats, or eliminate food service.

Major carriers offer similar service and similar frequent traveler programs. Their brands have become largely indistinguishable, with corporate colors, boarding passes, and flight attendants' uniforms all looking pretty much alike. Three major carriers, American, United, and Delta, use some variation of red, white, and blue in their brand identities. When USAir changed its name to US Airways in 1997, it embarked on a brand identity change that included repainting its planes to look strikingly similar to United's planes. Not surprisingly, Stephen M. Wolf, formerly of United, became US Airways' chairman in 1996.

The major carriers are brands that swim in a microcosmic version of the sea of gray. It's not surprising that bankruptcy has become a way of doing business. Yet it also has created an opportunity for another set of competitors—low-cost carriers—to enter the market. These breakaway brands—most notably, first Southwest Airlines and later JetBlue—are dramatically reshaping the industry:

> The growth of low cost carriers (LCCs) in the U.S. and elsewhere is arguably the single most important factor currently shaping the airline industry. While LCCs accounted for 7% of U.S. domestic passengers in 1990, their geographic scope was fairly limited, and for the most part, LCC service was synonymous with a single carrier, Southwest Airlines. In contrast, LCCs collectively accounted for nearly one-quarter of all domestic origin and destination (O&D) passengers during the first half of 2002.[4]

Launched in 1971, Southwest Airlines today flies some 65 million passengers annually and has been profitable each year. In 2002, JetBlue achieved the highest operating margin of any domestic U.S. airline and today has some 18 million customers.

The low-cost carriers are breakaway brands that have captured the attention of passengers and major carriers alike. Some of the major carriers have fought back by forming their own look-alike LCC brands, such as Delta's Song and United's Ted. But so far they haven't taken off—perhaps because they are nothing more than me-too brands.

Breakaway Brands Work Hard at Breaking Away

Product marketers in the food industry, hungry for increased sales, jump on the low-carb bandwagon.

CPG companies, chomping at the bit for more shelf space, extend their branded product lines.

Major airline carriers, seeing their market share take a nose-dive, launch their own low-fare alternatives to compete with the low cost carriers.

Is this the best way to differentiate and break away? Are look-alike products and me-too brands really necessary? Consumers today are discriminating, sophisticated buyers—and they are deciding the fate of brands with their wallets.

To meet the needs of the new consumer, it takes a new breed of company run by people who believe in brands that are exceptionally differentiated—brands that separate from their competition, and amaze and delight consumers. In some cases, these breakaway brands start entirely new categories.

To meet the needs of the new consumer, it takes a new breed of company run by people who believe in brands that are exceptionally differentiated— brands that separate from their competition, and amaze and delight consumers.

Some Breakaway Brands That Stand Out in the Sea of Gray

Absolut	Nike
Altoids	Royal Caribbean
Apple	Silk
Dell	Starbucks
eBay	Target
Gatorade	Titleist
JetBlue	Virgin Mobile
MINI	Volkswagen
Newman's Own	

Breakaway brands are still a tiny percentage of the brand world, but most of them are notoriously successful. For example:

- JetBlue is a breakaway brand airline that undercut the industry's pricing model while providing exceptional customer service and unexpected extras, like leather seats and satellite TV.

- Dell is a breakaway brand computer manufacturer, the first to successfully mass-customize and sell computers directly to the end user.

- Volkswagen is a breakaway brand auto manufacturer, carving out a market for German-engineered cars that are fun to drive but without the sticker shock.

- Starbucks is a breakaway brand retailer that created a new cachet for coffee.

- Royal Caribbean Cruise Lines is a breakaway brand provider of vacation experiences that have redefined the cruising industry.

- Newman's Own is a breakaway brand food products manufacturer that leverages a celebrity to sell products, and then donates its profits to charity.

Breakaway brands like these take risks, make sacrifices, hone their brand truth, and work hard at breaking away.

CLASSIC BREAKAWAY BRAND #1: APPLE

In 1976, two geeks, Steve Wozniak and Steve Jobs, start a renegade company with an implausible goal: to build "a computer for the rest of us." In 1984, Apple introduces the Macintosh, the first affordable personal computer with a graphical user interface, which becomes the model for Microsoft Windows-based PCs. That same year, Apple runs one of the most famous TV commercials ever, just a single time, to dramatize its uniqueness. "1984" depicts a woman runner who disrupts a Big Brother–style corporate meeting by smashing a large television screen, a pointed reference to "Big Blue" (IBM).

Apple never overtakes the traditional Microsoft Windows-based PC market, yet the quirky company continues to grow an iconic brand that owns a consumer perception for innovation and style. It develops a reputation for the quality and award-winning design of its products. Its marketing keeps pace with clean, sophisticated communications and advertising.

Apple becomes not just a brand, but a cultural icon. Defined by a new generation of computer users, Apple gets on the road to immortality early by aggressively placing its products in schools. (While one could argue this is a noble endeavor, it is also brilliant branding at work. What better way to influence the purchasing habits of youth than to expose them to your brand in the place where they spend the largest portion of their lives?)

Apple breaks away several more times as it evolves, continuing its youth appeal and product innovation with the introduction of the PowerBook, the iMac, and iMovie. Then Apple moves bravely into new territory as it introduces the iPod, a player that distinguishes the company as the leader in digital music. Apple follows that with the ingeniously timed iTunes. This low-cost music download service launches just as the legal controversy surrounding free music downloading is reaching its peak. iTunes sells more than 70 million songs in its first year. It now features the largest legal music download catalog available.

Apple continues its upward spiral in early 2005, when it introduces a $99 version of the iPod and a $499 iMac. The company's fiscal first-quarter profit for the period ending December 25, 2004, is four times higher on net income that reached $295 million, up from $63 million one year prior.

Here is a company that is turning breakaway products into breakaway profits.

It is more than the power of the brand that turned Apple into a breakaway company. Apple's leadership under breakaway CEO Steve Jobs, its tireless product innovation, and its bold and timely move into the digital music world have combined to reposition the company and keep Apple a fresh and colorful brand that uses its cachet to break away.

Just as important, Apple partnered with a smart, bold agency (TBWA\Chiat\Day) that helped the company pioneer breakaway advertising such as the "1984" ad referenced above, and the "Think Different" campaign, which marked the start of the Apple brand's reinvention.

As *BusinessWeek* said in its August 2003 special report on Apple, "morphing into a consumer-electronics company also capitalizes on a hip brand—the cult of cool—that Apple has spent billions building."

CLASSIC BREAKAWAY BRAND #2: NIKE

Equally cult-like is the Nike brand. In 1962, Bill Bowerman and Phil Knight found a company, Blue Ribbon Sports, that brings Japanese high-tech athletic shoes into the U.S. in an effort to combat the hold Germany had on the market. That doesn't last long. Founders Bowerman and Knight have something larger in mind—to create newly designed athletic shoes.

In 1970, Bowerman uses his wife's waffle iron to experiment with a rubber compound, creating a sole that is the forerunner, literally, of the modern running shoe. In 1971, the "swoosh" design comes into being, and in 1972, the company is renamed Nike, for the Greek winged goddess of victory.

Early on, Nike pioneers the concept of using athletic endorsements to build brand awareness and credibility. It lends an aura to Nike that will last for decades. The company gets American record-holding runner Steve Prefontaine to wear Nike brand shoes in the 1972 U.S. Olympic trials. By 1974, Nike's "waffle trainer" shoe is the best-selling training shoe in the country.

From this foundation, Nike grows exponentially by entering and dominating other sports markets, using high-profile athletes to build the brand. In 1978, Nike storms the tennis market by signing John McEnroe, whose personality typifies the cachet of the brand. On the road to success, Nike continuously innovates in ways that lead and shape its industry. As early as 1979, the company introduces a shoe with "Nike Air," a technologically advanced, patented air-sole cushioning system. It is the first of many future innovations that keep the company on the leadership edge.

In 1985, the basketball world succumbs to Nike as the Air Jordan line, endorsed by superstar Michael Jordan, is born. The "Just do it" campaign is launched in 1988, creating a buzz for Nike that lasts to this day. The company took a risk and partnered with a small local agency, Wieden + Kennedy. Dan Wieden came up with this tag line, one of the most famous in advertising history, and the agency went on to share in Nike's success. In 1990, Nike innovates again by opening Niketown in Portland, Oregon, the industry's first pure sports retail store.

Name any major sport, and chances are Nike is a dominant player. Lance Armstrong is a Nike athlete. Tiger Woods won three Majors using Nike golf balls. That's because Nike's core positioning is that the brand stands for the serious athlete, not the spectator. Sports is a metaphor for life, linking the cultures of the world. Nike never forgets that, and neither does its customers.

Over the years, Nike continues to improve its basic product—athletic footwear—and expands into athletic wear and equipment. Nike puts its imprint on the world in noble endeavors as well. One example is the company's "Reuse-A-Shoe" Program.

In 1991, some Nike employees wonder what happens to worn-out and defective athletic shoes. They learn that these products often end up in landfills. This realization inspires Nike to start Reuse-A-Shoe in 1993, recycling its first pair of sports footwear, with the intention of grinding it up for use in sports surfaces around the planet. By 2003, Nike rounds up, grinds up, and recycles 15 million pairs of post-consumer and defective athletic shoes (Nike and others).

Reuse-A-Shoe is more than a public relations campaign. Nike develops an economically feasible way to create and license "Nike Grind," returning shoes to their component parts and giving them a new life. Through Reuse-A-Shoe, Nike helps donate more than 150 sports surfaces to communities around the world.

Why? To increase the participation of young people in physical activity to help improve their lives—a goal that fits perfectly with the company's mission.

Today Nike is the dominant athletic footwear and sportswear company in the world, finishing its FY 2003 with revenues of $10.7 billion. Its "swoosh" logo and "Just do it" slogan are universally recognized. They are representative of the aspiration and connection between athletes, not merely promotional techniques.

Nike markets to, at, about, and for the serious athlete. The company hires athletes and employees who are tough, irreverent brand lovers. Nike teaches retailers how to market sports, not just products. These are just some of the reasons Nike is a breakaway brand. It is better known and better marketed than its rival Reebok, and the difference in sales and profits is a dramatic demonstration of Nike's success. (See Chapter 10 for the proof.)

BUILDING A BREAKAWAY BRAND ISN'T EASY

It isn't easy for brands like Apple and Nike to break away. Each company has made sacrifices, discarding ideas, products, and even people along the way. Each company has had to focus with laser-like clarity on its brand truth. In the case of Apple, it has meant reinvention; for Nike, it has been the relentless pursuit of performance. It takes vision, guts, and determination—and no small amount of risk.

These are the breakaway brands—brands like Apple and Nike—that have the long-term potential to succeed. These are the brands that are the most fun to run, the brands that bring in the most revenue, the brands that become cultural icons and win a special place in the hearts of consumers, competitors, and investors. These are the brands that stand out in the sea of gray, distinguishing themselves from all others.

The world needs—and consumers deserve—more breakaway brand success stories. Breakaway brands could mean growth in sales, profits, and a company's share price. CMOs could keep their jobs longer. And consumers could see advertising that really tells them why one brand is better than its competitors.

We've worked with hundreds of companies and we know one thing—it's the breakaway brands that succeed over the long haul. We'll show you how, as Nike would say, breakaway brands "Just do it."

Chapter 1 Break Points

- THINK ABOUT IT: Is there an over-population of me-too, look-alike brands? Which brands do you think stand out from the crowd successfully? Are marketers doing a good job of differentiating their brands? If you represented a brand in an over-crowded category, what would you do to break away?

- Consumers think brands are converging or becoming less distinct. Very few brands rise above commodity status.

- Brand proliferation is running rampant. Most brands follow rather than lead.

- The continuing expansion of brand choice creates a paradox—the reduction of the consumer's ability to make choices.

- Eighty percent of brands are merely treading water in a sea of gray. Only 20 percent are making waves.

- Brands, like the companies that create them, typically run in herds.

- It takes a new breed of company run by people who believe in brands that are exceptionally differentiated—brands that separate from their competition, and amaze and delight consumers.

- Breakaway brands are still a tiny percentage of the brand world, but most of them are notoriously successful.

- It is breakaway brands that have the long-term potential to succeed. These are the brands that stand out in the sea of gray, distinguishing themselves from all others.

CHAPTER 2

The Breakaway Brand

Before we attempt to define the essence of the breakaway brand, we should define the difference between a "brand" and a "branded product." Typically, we refer to a "brand" as a company name, such as Apple or Nike. But sometimes we may use "brand" to mean a "branded product." A product may have the same name as its parent company (Coca-Cola is both the company name and the name of one of the company's products). A product can also be individually branded ("Tide"), closely associated with its parent brand ("Honda Accord"), or several steps away from the brand ("Sprite, a product of Coca-Cola"). The result is, when we discuss a breakaway brand, we may be referring to a breakaway company or a breakaway product.

A Breakaway Brand "Thinks Different"

We consider Apple a breakaway brand. It turns out Apple has also manufactured its share of breakaway branded products, such as iMac and iPod.

Arnold Worldwide was pitching the Apple advertising account just before Steve Jobs returned to Apple in 1997 as interim CEO. The company was in the throes of a significant downturn in market share, stock value, and employee morale. When Jobs came back, he recognized the need to turn Apple around and re-create it as the breakaway brand it once was. He changed everything: He tore up all the plans and started over.

Steve Jobs ended the agency review and rehired Apple's previous ad agency, Chiat/Day (now TBWA\Chiat\Day). Jobs and Lee Clow, the agency's chief creative officer, had partnered on Apple's earlier successes. Jobs challenged the agency to help Apple get its focus back. Apple's new advertising campaign was centered around the theme, "Think Different." Rather than promoting computers, the campaign showed images of Einstein, Picasso, Gandhi, and other luminaries who, by "thinking different," changed the world. Apple was celebrating these great thinkers and, by association, identified itself as a company that could think different. The campaign won numerous advertising awards and brought Apple to the forefront again.

This was just one element in the reinvention of Apple. In 1997 Jobs announced that Apple would sell direct to the consumer through its online channel, The Apple Store. The following year, the company introduced the iMac, an oddly shaped computer available in various colors and aimed squarely at the Internet-connected consumer market. The iMac itself became a breakaway brand—the country's best-selling computer in the fall of 1998.

In retrospect, the iMac was the first innovative foray into a market that would later be receptive to the company's growing consumer presence. In 2001 Apple began opening retail Apple Stores, and by 2004 had opened some 80 of them worldwide. Apple's iPod/iTunes brands have spawned a new segment of fanatical fans—not only computer users but youthful members of the digital music generation. The iPod is an accessory in the Volkswagen Beetle and is integrated into BMW automobiles. With dominant market share, the iPod has become the de facto digital music standard.

With the "Think Different" campaign, Lee Clow and his agency produced work that distinguished Apple once again and set it on a course that led to the company's re-birth. Apple and its long-standing agency continue to "think different" today as they promote the wildly successful iPod.

This turning point—when Apple became Apple again—required the vision, guts, and risk-taking of a breakaway CEO like Steve Jobs. Tough decisions had to be made. A new direction had to be explained to employees, customers, and shareholders. Jobs took on the challenge and became a master builder of a breakaway brand.

Another master brand builder is Nike's former CEO, Phil Knight. He partnered with a relatively unknown agency, Wieden + Kennedy, to help create an image and advertising for what is today one of the world's most recognized brands. Dan Wieden is credited with coming up with the phrase "Just do it" in 1988—considered one of the most memorable tag lines in advertising. Wieden + Kennedy has been an active, valued partner in the Nike success story ever since.

Nike has its own set of fanatics: a wide variety of athletes around the world who "just do it." Nike has engendered a fierce loyalty from amateur and professional athletes alike, in virtually every sport. As if to confirm this dominance, Nike has purchased the rights to show its famous "swoosh" logo on the uniforms of collegiate and professional sports teams.

But Nike's magic extends beyond the dedicated athlete to the average consumer. People buy and wear the Nike brand as a symbol of belonging, whether or not they are active in sports. The Nike brand is representational of a broader spirit, a dedication to excellence, a way of life. As a breakaway brand, Nike is the gold standard.

Apple and Nike are full of color, texture, and vitality. They have a richness and vibrancy about them. They take risks, forging ahead into new territories. They are not trend-followers, they are trendsetters.

Apple and Nike are cultural icons, companies that have the ability to establish emotional connections with their target audiences. They are perceived to be natural born leaders. What seems to come naturally to Apple and Nike is far from it, however; breakaway brands such as these are carefully created, marketed, and positioned to stand out in a sea of gray.

Breakaway brands are carefully created, marketed, and positioned to stand out in a sea of gray.

A Breakaway Brand Is Positioned for Success

The classic book *Positioning: The Battle for Your Mind*, by Al Ries and Jack Trout (McGraw-Hill, 2000), introduced a new idea: the notion that a product's success is based on how it is *positioned* in the mind of the prospect, not on the attributes the product may have.

The book cites an excellent example of the power of positioning: Avis versus Hertz in the car rental market. Avis positioned itself as number 2 with the realization that it would never displace number-1 Hertz. By acknowledging its secondary position, and by reinforcing that position with the underdog slogan, "We try harder," Avis drove a wedge between the two companies (Hertz and Avis) and every other competitor, creating a "category of two." Avis now owns the number-2 position and has maintained its "second only to Hertz" perception for many years. The famous "We try harder" slogan, created in 1963, is still used by Avis today.

Positioning presents a different kind of challenge in the modern brand world. At a time when consumer desire and demand drives marketing, brand positioning can determine product adoption and success. The problem is that too many brands are jockeying to position themselves just right. Most product categories already have leaders, so a new brand coming into the category must find a counter-position to succeed. The alternatives are to create a subset of the category by appealing to a smaller audience segment, or create an entirely new category. Either way, positioning takes on a whole new meaning.

At a time when consumer desire and demand drives marketing, brand positioning can determine product adoption and success.

BRAND NAMES CAN BECOME CATEGORY NAMES

First movers who define product categories are difficult to displace. Consider the brands Coca-Cola, Kleenex, and FedEx. Each of these brands has become synonymous with the product it represents. In these commonplace phrases, notice how the product category, in brackets, is substituted in conversation by the brand name:

"I'll have a Coke [cola]."

"Please get me a Kleenex [tissue]."

"Let's FedEx [overnight] that to the client."

While usage of brand names in this context is the worst nightmare of trademark attorneys, nothing could be better to a brand marketer than tip-of-the-tongue consumer awareness. These brand names are indicative of a lofty position bestowed upon only a handful of brands. They are so tightly positioned as leaders within their categories that they have woven themselves into the fabric of American life.

When used in conversation, most everyone would recognize an entire product category by these brand names. Each brand is deeply ingrained in the consumer's mind, regardless of its competition.

First movers such as Coke, Kleenex, and FedEx are original breakaway brands. But even these iconic brands can be vulnerable to breakaway competition if they aren't careful. The marketplace is changing, and brand marketers are becoming more aggressive. Consumers are not as brand loyal as they once were, and that leaves the door open for new breakaway brands. Pepsi has gained on Coke in recent years, Kleenex has fallen prey to price-cutting competitors, and UPS (and, more recently DHL) have fought for—and won—market share from FedEx.

The Top 25 Brands

According to *Business Week* (August 1, 2005), these are the world's top 25 brands in terms of value. Many, but not all, are breakaway brands.

1. Coca-Cola	14. American Express
2. Microsoft	15. Gillette
3. IBM	16. BMW
4. GE	17. Cisco
5. Intel	18. Louis Vuitton
6. Nokia	19. Honda
7. Disney	20. Samsung
8. McDonald's	21. Dell
9. Toyota	22. Ford
10. Marlboro	23. Pepsi
11. Mercedes	24. Nescafe
12. Citibank	25. Merrill Lynch
13. Hewlett-Packard	

COKE...IS IT STILL THE REAL THING?

Let's take a look at how a brand like Coca-Cola first reaches breakaway brand status—and then finds itself facing new challenges.

Coca-Cola is arguably the greatest American brand of all time. *BusinessWeek* ranks Coca-Cola as the world's most valuable brand, worth almost $70 billion.[1] Coca-Cola is present in over 200 countries, marketing more than 300 individual brands worldwide, but the Coca-Cola brand is certainly the most renowned. More than 70 percent of the Coca-Cola Company's income comes from outside the United States.

But is Coke still the real thing? While it has long been regarded as a breakaway brand, it is far from invulnerable. In fact, in the last several years, Coke seems to have faltered. The brand has been increasingly under attack from direct and indirect beverage competitors.

Coke's story starts with history and a heritage—and depends on the ongoing usage of smart brand promotion and advertising.

The product was first invented in 1886; "Coca-Cola" became a registered trademark in 1893. Coke maintained its brand leadership through decades of enormous change, surviving at least one major brand gaffe, the introduction of "New Coke."

Coca-Cola's logo, dominant red color, and packaging have remained part of the brand since the beginning. The Coca-Cola bottle has achieved worldwide fame, becoming a collector's item in its own right. While "Coke" was trademarked in 1945, and the company has used different typographic approaches to label its products, the brand identity continues to be strong and recognizable from one product variation to another.

Coca-Cola credits Robert Woodruff, who became the company's president in 1923, with having the marketing vision to grow the brand into a worldwide powerhouse. Woodruff connected Coca-Cola with the U.S. Olympic team of 1928 and put the brand logo on such places as dog racing sleds in Canada and bull-fighting rings in Spain. During his tenure, the company introduced a breakaway packaging idea, the six-pack, to dramatically increase product distribution and consumption.

In 1931 Coca-Cola used an illustrated Santa Claus in its advertising, capturing in portrait America's interpretation of the mythical character—and endearing millions to the brand. Santa would continue to appear in Coca-Cola's advertising for decades to come.

During World War II, in a stroke of promotional genius, Woodruff insisted that "every man in uniform gets a bottle of Coca-Cola for five cents, wherever he is, and whatever it costs the Company." In 1950 Coca-Cola became the first-ever product to appear on the cover of *Time* magazine.

Coca-Cola managed to break away once again when it introduced the 12-ounce can in 1960 and lift-top cans in 1964, repackaging the soda for a new kind of on-the-go consumption. In 1985 Coca-Cola became the first soft drink ever in space.

Today Coca-Cola's use of brand promotion reinforces the brand day in, day out. The company has been a leader in creating buzz—its identity appears on soda fountains and in menus, on glasses and on clocks, and on cups in sports arenas throughout the world. One of its recent innovative initiatives is the six-story "digital communications portal" (a.k.a. electronic billboard) featuring 32 custom-made high-definition LED screens, in New York City's Times Square. Described by the company as an "advertising sculpture," the billboard carries custom-created digital imagery about Coke that can be changed on a moment's notice.

PEPSI: A CHALLENGER BRAND EMERGES

How could any brand possibly challenge such a powerhouse as Coca-Cola? The chink in Coke's armor has been another cola, itself over 100 years old. This brand adopted a marketing strategy that, over many years, has ever so slightly eroded Coke's dominance. The brand is Pepsi-Cola, of course.

As early as 1963, Pepsi positioned itself against Coke with the slogan, the "Pepsi Generation" and the ad headline, "For those who think young." Over the decades, Pepsi has continued to associate itself with a younger audience, implying that Coke is old-fashioned and behind the times. Pepsi has employed youthful celebrities, run brash ads during the Super Bowl, and directly challenged Coca-Cola with taste tests.

While Pepsi has never overtaken Coke, it has been a persistent marketer with a consistent message and, as such, has accomplished much the same thing as Avis did with Hertz. Most consumers would place Pepsi in the same two-cola category as Coca-Cola. And Pepsi has slowly but surely gained market share on its archrival.

Coca-Cola has fought back with its own youth-oriented strategies. The company launched a new variation of the Sprite soda brand called "Sprite Remix" in 2003, for example. Targeting the urban youth audience, the word "Remix" was chosen to tie into remixed music. Coca-Cola announced it would position the brand as a true "remix," changing the flavor every so often to keep it new.

Nonetheless, Pepsi has dulled some of Coke's former luster. But both brands are vulnerable to the brand proliferation problem we referenced in Chapter 1. Coca-Cola's "C2," a 2004 brand born of the low-carb craze, has generally been regarded by industry experts as a failure. In May 2005, a year after its introduction, Pepsi officially dropped "Pepsi Edge." Launched as a mid-calorie cola, "Pepsi Edge" failed to find a place between regular Pepsi and Diet Pepsi. Consumers just didn't buy it.

GATORADE: A NEW DRINK CATEGORY EMERGES

To complicate matters for Coca-Cola and Pepsi-Cola, the beverage market has changed with the consumer. No longer fixated on colas, consumers have demanded entirely new categories to quench their thirst. Now other beverages are better connecting with the consumers' wants and needs than the colas, and they are the ones becoming the breakaway brands.

> *Now other beverages are better connecting with the consumers' wants and needs than the colas, and they are the ones becoming the breakaway brands.*

Gatorade, for example, grew out of a need for athletes to rehydrate themselves during strenuous physical activity. Named after the University of Florida Gators, the product was proven to help replace fluid and electrolytes in players.

Gatorade launched its brand with this fact in mind and now relies on four brand building blocks, according to the company:

1. **SCIENTIFIC INTEGRITY** Gatorade has made a concerted effort to validate its claims through its Sports Science Institute. This stuff works, and Gatorade can prove it.

2. **FIELD OF PLAY** Gatorade's strategy is to dominate field sports and literally be on the sidelines, assuring that the best athletes use it on the right occasion. When the winning football coach is doused by his players on the sideline, every consumer knows it's a Gatorade bath.

3. **IT'S FOR ME**   This is a product that is really designed for an athlete who wants to be at his or her best. Gatorade is a sports drink with a purpose—when you sweat, you need it to replenish the fluids in your body.

4. **BROAD AVAILABILITY**   Gatorade is easy to find in stores, despite its specialized nature. Purchased by Pepsi in 2001, the beverage will use Pepsi's distribution channels to expand from 15 countries to more than 100.

Gatorade sponsors the NFL and is the official sports drink of most professional sports leagues and associations. The beverage currently has 82.5 percent of the sports drink market and its competitor, Powerade, has 13.5 percent market share, as reported in *Advertising Age* (May 2, 2005). How fitting it is that Powerade is marketed by Coca-Cola. Here, then, the tables are turned: In the sports drink category, Pepsi dominates and Coke is a distant second.

A Breakaway Brand Continuously Innovates

For brands like Coca-Cola and Pepsi-Cola to maintain their leadership, they need to introduce (or acquire) new products and think of new ways to keep their brands top-of-mind. They must bring ever-changing excitement to soft drink brands that otherwise could lose their fizz.

This kind of continuous innovation is a key quality of the breakaway brand. Bain & Company conducted a study of 524 brands across 100 categories and found just two indicators that led to a brand beating its category's growth each year from 1997 to 2001: *product innovation* and *advertising*. In "Making Cool Brands Hot" (*Harvard Business Review*, June 2003), Bain's John

Blasberg and Vijay Vishwanath observe that "winning innovators cropped up in high- and low-growth categories and among brands that were new and mature, big and small, premium and value, leaders and followers."

Bain & Company conducted a study of 524 brands across 100 categories and found just two indicators that led to a brand beating its category's growth: **product innovation** *and* **advertising**.

Breakaway brands are those that continually innovate and advertise. Bain & Company's study implies that a great brand cannot rest on its laurels, because it could lose its dominance to a more innovative brand, or a brand that promotionally outspends it. Likewise, an unknown brand could catapult to the top of a category with strong product innovation and aggressive advertising. Over time, this lesser brand could itself become the category leader.

"AMERICAN IDOL" AS A BREAKAWAY BRAND

Unless you don't have teenagers or have been living on another planet, you know that "American Idol" is a Fox network program on which youthful contestants sing their hearts out to become the nation's next music sensation. Launched in the summer of 2002, "American Idol" started the 2004 season with over 28 million viewers, American TV's largest audience ever for a debut series. Its fourth season, which began in January 2005, again broke records, with the first show attracting over 33 million viewers— reportedly the third-highest rating in the Fox network's history.

Coca-Cola, by the way, recognized the youthful draw of "American Idol" and became an early primary sponsor of the show. Coke created a humorous and memorable television commercial that featured one of the judges from the show. But that was just part of the marketing plan—the company arranged to have its brand fully integrated into "American Idol." Oversized Coke tumblers prominently appear in front of the judges each week. The show features the "Coca-Cola Red Room," where Idol contestants chat with the host before performing. Coca-Cola runs special promotions that tie in with the show; at the conclusion of the first season, the company offered the red couches from the Red Room as prizes in a contest. Not a bad way to fight that "old-fashioned product" image.

Other sponsors have recognized the halo effect of "American Idol." The show has strategically used promotional partnerships with brands that fit its audience's profile. "American Idol" legitimized cellular phone text messaging by accepting text-messaged votes from the public via AT&T Wireless cellular phones. The cell phone service provider created a sweepstakes tie-in that gave individuals who voted via text messaging the chance to win idol-like treatment in New York or Beverly Hills. Cory Kallet, senior partner at Einson Freeman, the promotion agency that worked with AT&T Wireless, says the partnership paid off:

> The vast majority of AT&T Wireless customers have text-capable handsets but were not using this feature. By incentivizing them—via the sweeps and ability to vote and get "American Idol" content—we were able to significantly increase the number of subscribers who tried texting, which was the primary way for them to participate.[2]

AT&T enhanced its presence with TV, radio, print, online, and point-of-purchase media. Kallet says that more than 5 million people were identified as repeat text-messaging voters as a result of the promotion and sweepstakes. Now, with the Cingular–AT&T Wireless merger, Cingular is reaping the benefits of associating with the show. According to research firm comScore Networks, Cingular's web site traffic increased

74 percent from the first "American Idol" show in January to the season finale in May 2005.

"American Idol" is itself a colorful and brilliantly executed breakaway brand. From the stylish pop-star logo to the perfectly integrated web site, "American Idol" is a model of what a brand franchise can become. Once the television season ends, "American Idol" extends its brand by sponsoring national tours featuring the show's finalists. Finalists' and the winners' CDs, as well as T-shirts, jewelry, and an "official American Idol phone," are available for sale on the web site and through retail stores.

"American Idol" has had a significant impact on the music business. Every season's winners, and several of the finalists, have seen their songs skyrocket to the top of the pop music charts. Contestants have appeared in other television shows and starred in movies. And every time they do, millions of teenagers can't help but recall the "American Idol" television show.

If you have any doubt about this brand's sustainability, consider the fact that "American Idol" ended its fourth season in May 2005 as the top television show once again. The program garnered 500 million votes for contestants during the season, and was largely responsible for Fox Network's finish in 2005 as the leading television network.

A Breakaway Brand Connects with Its Audience

A breakaway brand forms an emotional connection with its audience. The brand owner understands the role that brand plays in the lives of consumers and makes sure the brand's attributes match up with the target consumers' needs.

"American Idol" works because it brilliantly targets its youth audience. Its contestants are youthful, its host is youthful, its sponsors' commercials are youthful. "American Idol" is more than a television show—it is a lifestyle experience, a kind of "Who Wants to Be a Millionaire" for the teen generation. It merchandises itself in a way that its audience finds acceptable—even if it seems crassly commercialized. "American Idol" is a breakaway brand that its target audience can respect and admire. It even crosses over to older generations—parents tend to watch the show with their children because it gives them something to talk about. Moreover, "American Idol" is a brand that truly empowers its audience. After all, it is viewers who, with their votes, select the next American idol.

As "American Idol" demonstrates, a breakaway brand has a firm grip on the nature of its audience—its needs, its desires, its buying patterns. The great breakaway brand is even capable of expanding that audience to remain vibrant.

DISNEY

Disney became a great differentiated brand by marketing creativity and magic to children. We remember as kids gathering around the television every Sunday evening to watch the "Wonderful World of Disney"—an early example of advertainment, a concept introduced in Chapter 1.

But Disney has had to keep up with the times. While it still markets to children, Disney has continued to grow by marketing to children's parents and grandparents—really, to the child in all of us.

Disney is a brand with subbrands: its characters. Whether youngsters are at a Disney theme park, on a Disney cruise ship, or shopping for Disney merchandise, they will find a character they know and love. Characters are reinforced in every Disney theme park gift shop, in every television show on the Disney Channel, and in every Disney movie. Disney has turned movies like "The Lion King" into franchises that generate millions of dollars of additional revenue through promotional tie-ins with restaurant chains, spin-off animated television series, an award-winning Broadway show, and toys.

The company is not just about character brands, however. What Disney really does is create one giant entertainment event. Disney employees are called "cast members." Every Disney locale is a stage. All communications and customer touch points are integrated. Every possible guest interface is carefully scripted. Disney properties are clean and safe. Customer expectations are not just met, but often exceeded. This is a breakaway brand that, at its core, represents what every child and their parents want.

The Disney brand is not without its share of challenges, however. For one thing, the venerable Mickey Mouse, long Disney's "leading mouse," is now over 75 years old. Disney had to wonder if the character still had relevance—and selling power. In 2002 Disney created a secret war room filled with Mickey Mouse merchandise of all types.[3] Disney executives visited it in an effort to reinvigorate the Mickey character. By late 2002, Disney had introduced retro-style Mickey Mouse T-shirts that caught on with celebrities and became hot sellers in boutiques. While the famous mouse had been endearing to an older generation, this reawakening interest was evidence of Mickey's resilience in changing times.

In 2004 Mickey Mouse and other Disney characters began appearing on U.S. postage stamps. In the fall of 2004, Disney entered the computer market with a "Disney Dream Desk PC" targeting 6- to 11-year-olds; the monitor is in the shape of giant Mickey Mouse ears.

While some would say Disney is not the breakaway brand it once was, its universal appeal is undeniable. Consumers young and old from around the globe believe in the "Disney magic." The broader Disney audience is comprised of children, their brothers and sisters, their parents, and their grandparents. These individuals could vary in gender, income, race, religion, and even country of origin, but they all love Disney.

STARBUCKS

Starbucks has been the subject of numerous brand studies and books, so we won't cover it extensively here. But as a legendary breakaway brand, the company should not be overlooked.

Starbucks dispels any doubt that it is possible to penetrate the global market with a commodity product. The Starbucks brand is arguably the single most recognized coffee brand in the world. As a breakaway brand, Starbucks' real winning proposition is bringing quality and variety to away-from-home coffee. By capturing the consumer trend to small indulgences, and emphasizing the feeling of community in its shops and in the company's involvement in local causes, Starbucks catapulted to brand stardom.

Anne Saunders, Senior Vice President of Marketing, details five reasons why Starbucks has achieved such success[4]:

- *Everything sources from the company's core values.* Saunders says that each year, Starbucks surveys its 70,000 employees in the U.S. and finds that over 80 percent of the respondents understand the company's values. Starbucks provides a great work environment and fosters respect and dignity.

- *Never compromise quality.* Starbucks is obsessive about quality, says Saunders. The company buys locally from some

600 farmers and constantly samples coffee throughout the entire supply chain.

- *Human connection.* Starbucks emphasizes the human side of its business with its employees, its suppliers, and its customers. On the customer side, for example, each Starbucks retail location is encouraged to connect with the local community. Through the "Make Your Mark" program, workers and customers work side by side to service the community.

- *Stay fresh through innovation.* Starbucks tries to anticipate things customers haven't thought of, Saunders says. The company also listens to customers—for example, now 80 percent of Starbucks' stores have wireless, largely because of customer requests.

- *Take the road less traveled.* Starbucks spent less than $10 million in advertising in its first ten years. Instead, the company invests in local grassroots promotions and strives for impact over efficiency. Starbucks will try nontraditional ideas that are aligned with its core values. For example, in 2005 the company rolled out a program called "The Way I See It," featuring provocative thoughts in 65 words or fewer from authors, celebrities, and thought leaders. Each thought is printed on one of Starbucks' 800 million coffee cups. The purpose, says Saunders, is to promote a national dialogue, and to get people to stop and think.

Starbucks uses its great retail presence as a strong promotional technique; after all, in some cities, Starbucks locations seem as pervasive as ATMs. It is this intense level of market penetration, along with its community outreach, that contributes to the brand's remarkable awareness. Anne Saunders says that

Starbucks never pays for product placement in television or the movies—but they get their share of it anyway. A huge Starbucks coffee cup was featured in the movie *Shrek 2*, for example.

Starbucks is also a brand that has successfully transitioned from storefront to grocery store shelf. Starbucks coffee, ice cream, and bottled Frappuccino are widely available for consumer purchase. In February 2005, in agreement with Jim Beam, Starbucks even introduced a branded coffee liqueur. The liqueur will not be available in Starbucks retail locations, but rather in restaurants, bars, and liquor stores.

This product is a particularly intriguing brand extension, because the company's research found that Starbucks customers are nine times more likely than the national average to drink coffee liqueurs.[5] While Kahlua has been the dominant brand in this category, Starbucks Coffee Liqueur will surely appeal to the 30 million customers worldwide who visit a Starbucks store each week.

An important point to make is that Starbucks is a premium priced product, and yet the company can raise its prices without much impact on sales. That's what a great breakaway brand can do. With constant attention to quality, the ability to introduce innovative products, a strong sense of community, and concern for social and environmental issues, Starbucks is a model of a breakaway brand every marketer admires.

A Breakaway Brand Establishes Leadership

Dell is a computer juggernaut. A direct marketer heavily dependent on Internet sales, Dell survived the dot-com crash and the technology meltdown. The company grew from $31.2 billion in sales in fiscal year (FY) 2002 to $35.4 billion in FY 2003 to

$41.4 billion in FY 2004. It is now the world's leading maker of PCs, having won a war fought against such powerhouses as IBM, Compaq, and HP. In 2005 Dell was named "America's Most Admired Company" by *FORTUNE* (March 7, 2005).

How did Dell become a breakaway brand that so definitively separated itself from everyone else? Its 2004 Annual Report contains the answer: "We define product leadership as bringing to market exactly what customers want, when they want it, for the best value in the industry." When it comes to something as sophisticated and complex as computers, this is no easy task.

Dell is a colorful breakaway brand in many ways, from its legendary college-dropout founder Michael Dell to its battle for PC superiority to its direct-to-the-consumer sales pitch. But it was Dell's ability to reinvent computer manufacturing that distinguished it from everyone else. Dell created a new business model: mass customizing computers and selling them direct to customers with no distributor, reseller, or retailer as the middleman. Dell's business model offers several significant competitive advantages:

- By selling directly and eliminating resellers, retailers, and other intermediaries, Dell can offer more powerful, better systems for less money than its competitors. The company has leveraged its strength in this area to enter new product categories, such as inkjet and laser printing.

- Every Dell system is built to order. Customers get exactly, and only, what they want. Dell extended the build-to-order strategy to the Internet and became a pioneer of online mass customization, developing efficient procurement, manufacturing, and distribution processes to do so. As a result, buyers can specify customized computer systems online, and Dell typically delivers them in fewer than 30 days.

- Dell provides tailored customer service, using knowledge gained from direct contact before and after the sale. Dell offers extensive online customer resources, such as Dell Premier web pages, a series of customized electronic storefronts/information portals for large customers. Premier.Dell.com allows users to configure their systems in real time, with up-to-date pricing for each organization. This information resource is directly connected to the customer's purchasing system for expedited ordering.

- Dell continuously innovates in its product lines. Its business model allows Dell to introduce the latest relevant technology much more quickly than through indirect distribution channels. Inventory is turned in ten days or fewer, on average.

- Dell stands in stark contrast to other computer manufacturers whose brands have been ravaged by technology change and industry consolidation.

A Moment of Silence for a Former Breakaway Brand

Do you remember a company named Digital Equipment Corporation (often shortened to "DEC")? Digital introduced the first minicomputer, taking IBM by surprise and the industry by storm. As a result, Digital had become the second-largest computer company in the world (IBM was number 1) by the late 1980s. The Digital brand was well known throughout the world; in fact, Digital tended to be even more highly regarded outside the United States than it was domestically. One could say that Digital, at this point in time, was a breakaway brand.

By the 1990s, however, Digital was in decline. Some believe the company had not kept up with technological change; others believe it was too large and lumbering; still others believe it ineffectively marketed its products. Whatever the reasons might be, the brand was mortally wounded. In 1998 Compaq Corporation acquired Digital Equipment Corporation.

Compaq was itself a breakaway brand, at its time the most successful IPO launch in history. An upstart that went head-to-head against IBM in the portable PC market, Compaq carved out a desirable and growing niche. But the notion that Compaq would grow large enough to acquire a company the size of Digital was virtually unthinkable. When it happened, Compaq soon sublimated the Digital brand. (Curiously, the Digital logo itself lives on, resurrected with permission by an IT services company operating in India called Digital GlobalSoft. From a practical perspective, though, Digital as a computer brand is gone.)

Swallowing the Digital behemoth wasn't easy for Compaq. It was a merger of two unlike entities in every way—Digital was a Massachusetts minicomputer manufacturer with a sophisticated networking arm, a global services business focused on large corporations, and a computer-chip manufacturing plant. It was a company started and run by engineers with a loose, disorganized matrix management structure.

Compaq was a hotshot Texas company that built its whole business on knocking off PC technology and making a better, smaller product at an attractive price. Culturally, Compaq had a drive and intensity that Digital lacked. And Compaq's brand perception was all about desktop PCs in the mind of the buyer (and the investor). With the Digital acquisition, Compaq's business suddenly included a different class of computers, enterprise-wide consulting services, and large-scale networking—an inventory of items completely foreign to the company's audience.

The Compaq brand no longer represented its core strength. There was sure to be brand confusion, perhaps even brand resentment. How could Compaq come to stand for something entirely different to the IT marketplace?

That problem didn't last long enough to be solved. In 2002 Compaq itself was acquired by Hewlett-Packard, better known as HP. (An interesting side note: HP and Digital were bitter rivals during Digital's heyday.) Yet another branding challenge was born—Compaq, which had acquired Digital, was itself being acquired by HP. Which brand would be dominant going forward? All customers had to do was look for a sign—literally.

In its home state of Massachusetts, Digital had a very strong physical presence. With the Compaq acquisition, Digital signs in front of buildings and office parks all over the state came down and were replaced with Compaq signs. Then, all the Compaq signs were replaced with HP signs.

So here is a company that went from the Massachusetts Miracle to the Texas Massacre to the Silicon Valley Savior. Clearly, the commitment to the Digital brand has ended (except in India!). The equity in the Digital brand is gone, the heritage of that brand all but forgotten. And while the Compaq brand exists as of this writing, we suspect the commitment to the Compaq brand will end as well. The equity in that brand will then be gone, the heritage of that brand all but forgotten, too. The HP brand will have the challenge of growing and succeeding despite all of this brand baggage it carries with it. As if to punctuate this tale, it was announced in February 2005 that HP's CEO, Carly Fiorina, resigned, reportedly under pressure from the company's board of directors.

The point of the story is not that Digital, a dying brand, should have been saved, or that Compaq, an acquired brand, should have been retained. Rather, it is to demonstrate what can happen to great brands, even breakaway brands, when they fail at positioning, do not innovate, do not know their audience, and do not establish brand leadership.

Chapter 2 Break Points

- THINK ABOUT IT: We've identified a few breakaway brands in this chapter, such as "American Idol," Dell, Disney, and Starbucks. We'll be discussing several more throughout the book. Are these the brands you first think of as "breaking away" from the rest? Think about those brands you believe truly separate themselves from all others. How do they do it? Why do they stand apart?

- Apple reinvented itself when it decided to "think different." Steve Jobs returned to Apple as its CEO and recognized the need to turn Apple back into the breakaway brand it once was.

- Positioning is the first critical element in the success of a breakaway brand.

- Today, brand positioning can determine product adoption and success. Most product categories already have leaders, so a new brand coming into the category must find a counter-position to succeed.

- First movers such as Coca-Cola, Kleenex, and FedEx may be the original breakaway brands, but they can be vulnerable to breakaway competition.

- Two indicators lead to a brand beating its category's growth each year: product innovation and advertising.

- A breakaway brand continuously innovates.

- A breakaway brand connects with its audience.

- A breakaway brand establishes leadership.

CHAPTER 3

The Process of Breaking Away

Too many brands focus on short-term gains at the expense of long-term goals. Many brand owners seem to be more concerned about quick profits than lasting value in the marketplace. All too often, effective advertising campaigns are abandoned long before they have run their course, just because the brand owner wants to try something new.

That's not how it should be. The breakaway brand strives for consistency and sustainability in both its product and its marketing. It begins with a brand marketer targeting a mindset and understanding how to communicate with that mindset—and everything goes through the mindset filter from that point forward. Brands like Apple, Nike, JetBlue, Volkswagen, and Mercedes-Benz stay true and consistent to the mindset with every promotional activity or advertising campaign.

Consistency at the product level is not always guaranteed. It is one thing for the quality of a tube of toothpaste to be consistent, but quite another for the quality of a luxury automobile to be consistent. Yet with a luxury car, it isn't just product quality that must be consistent—it is the entire *brand experience* that must be uncompromisingly consistent, from the quality of the car itself, to the consumer's experience at the point of sale, to the service provided by an authorized dealer, to the communications the consumer receives from corporate headquarters, to the advertising that the consumer may see or hear.

The more complex the brand, the harder it is to be consistent. Imagine the challenge for a hotel chain or restaurant brand to control the consistency of the brand experience at locations around the world.

A breakaway brand maintains its leadership position because consistency is a pervasive concept within the brand owner's organization. Consistency in brand values, in product attributes, in brand advertising. Consistency in the brand promise, or brand truth, and in targeting a winning mindset. Consistency must be part of the corporate commitment to the brand.

But don't read "consistency" as boring. Today's breakaway brands maintain a consistency in their brand truth, but they are not constrained by predictability—sometimes it's the brand's marketing that surprises, delights, and maybe even shocks the modern consumer into action. Young consumers in particular will accept a brand's originality in marketing as part of its personality. Virgin Mobile, referenced in Chapter 1, and the "truth" anti-smoking campaign, described in Chapter 5, are good examples of how brands can break the mold in marketing yet remain consistent at their core.

A breakaway brand maintains its leadership position because consistency is a pervasive concept within the brand owner's organization.

Consistency is also important because the more the consumer interacts with and understands a brand, the more aware the consumer becomes of the brand's competition. As Michael Porter says in his book *Competitive Strategy: Techniques for Analyzing Industries and Competitors* (Free Press, 1998), "Through repeat purchasing, buyers accumulate knowledge about a product, its use, and the characteristics of competing brands. Products have a tendency to become *more like commodities* over time as buyers become more sophisticated and purchasing tends to be based on better information."

Consistency breeds long-term commitment to the brand. In a product world where the next new thing tends to grab the most attention and advertising campaigns can change as quickly as the weather, committing to a brand through thick and thin is challenging. The level of commitment by the organization that owns the brand could determine the brand's sustainability. The CEO must truly "live the brand." (More about that in Chapter 9.) For example, Apple could not have reinvented itself without Steve Jobs living the brand.

The Breakaway Brand Is Based on a Strong Brand Truth

The brand truth is not marketing hype—it is the commitment of the brand's owner to the consumer, stated or implied, to make the brand *perform as promised*. For a brand to break away, the brand truth must be well articulated, strong, real, and unique to the brand. The consumer must find the brand truth completely believable—not false.

For a brand to break away, the brand truth must be strong, real, and unique to the brand. The consumer must find the brand truth completely believable—not false.

Brands that break away from others tend to develop truths that are consistent over a long period of time—truths based on promises that can be kept. A brand truth often begins with the perception of the brand itself. If the consumer has the perception that the brand is trustworthy, he or she is more likely to embrace the brand truth.

Often the brand truth is communicated via a mission statement to employees, and to the public via advertising, promotion, and packaging. The brand truth is typically captured by the brand's positioning statement, which in some cases is translated into a slogan or tag line—brief, memorable copy that is used in advertising campaigns.

A breakaway brand's truth is one that is almost universally recognized as its own and no one else's. Most consumers immediately think of a superior luxury automobile when they hear the word "Mercedes." Mercedes-Benz as a brand name is actually over 100 years old, yet today it remains one of the world's great premium brands. The three-pointed star that appears in a circle on the hood of the Mercedes-Benz car is perhaps better known as a symbol of luxury than the name itself.

Mercedes-Benz obtains lasting worldwide exposure by its involvement in numerous high-quality endeavors that support its brand promise. The company publishes *Mercedes-Benz Transport*, Europe's biggest commercial vehicle magazine; sponsors the "Laureus World Sports Awards" for outstanding athletes and partners with ATP, the worldwide organization for men's tennis; and sponsors the Fashion Weeks in New York and Australia. In 2003 Mercedes announced a joint venture with designer Giorgio Armani, resulting in the creation of the Mercedes-Benz CLK Giorgio Armani Design Car. The Mercedes reputation is unequalled—and that's the best example of a strong brand truth.

Mercedes-Benz is an admired, successful breakaway brand because its brand truth is strong. The company stays true to its promise of modern luxury throughout every element of its marketing mix. From its product designs to its advertising to its collateral materials to its dealerships, everything that bears the distinctive Mercedes-Benz star connotes quality, design, class, and consistency.

A WINNING BRAND TRUTH IS BOTH RATIONAL AND EMOTIONAL

The *rational* aspect of the brand truth appeals to the consumer's thought ("the mind"), while the *emotional* aspect appeals to the consumer's feeling ("the heart and soul"). If the brand truth can embody both the mind *and* the heart and soul, it will be a winning proposition—and a lasting one.

Mercedes-Benz's brand truth evokes both rational and emotional responses from an upscale consumer. There are rational reasons for purchasing this automobile: engineering, safety, service, quality. There are also emotional reasons: the prestige of being associated with a legendary luxury automobile, the feeling of security for the driver and his or her family, and the experience of driving it.

When rational and emotional elements are artfully blended, it can result in a very powerful brand truth—and a winning breakaway brand. Such is the case with Miller Lite. At the time of its national introduction in 1975, Miller Lite hit on a unique, breakaway brand truth: "Tastes Great. Less Filling." In fact, Miller Lite created a "category of one." Miller Lite found a way to appeal to the rational and emotional sides of beer drinkers at the same time: "I like to drink beer, but I know it has a lot of calories. I like the taste of beer, and I'm glad Miller Lite gives me that great taste. But it's less filling, which means it doesn't have as many calories, so I can still drink beer without worrying about gaining weight or feeling bloated."

When rational and emotional elements are artfully blended, it can result in a very powerful brand truth—and a winning breakaway brand.

Miller Brewing Company was the number 4 brewer in the United States at the time of Miller Lite's introduction. By 2004 its light beer brand had helped Miller rise to number 2. The brand instigated a revolution in beer as other makers rushed to introduce light beers. Over twenty years later, while the creative approaches have changed, Miller Lite's advertising still incorporates "Tastes Great. Less Filling." into its messaging—a lasting testament to the power of the brand truth.

The Breakaway Brand Targets a Winning Mindset

Earlier we discussed how breakaway companies like Apple, Nike, and Disney target audiences. We call that defining a mindset.

Precise audience targeting is becoming a necessity in an increasingly microsegmented world. But the breakaway brand is just as successful at cutting across demographics (age, gender, income, location) and psychographics (attitudes, values, opinions) to reach a broader audience. The breakaway brand appeals to a *winning mindset* that articulates the attitude of the brand's best customers and prospects. The winning mindset is where the brand truly connects with the audience, forming both a rational and emotional connection with the right individual.

CRUISING ALONG TO SUCCESS

Here's a case of how a cruise line discovered a winning mindset and, in so doing, broke away and redefined the cruising industry.

In the mid- to late '90s, the cruise industry found itself challenged by changing market conditions. Several decades of conservative, me-too marketing campaigns had convinced about 10 percent of the American public that cruising was a nice, convenient, affordable way to spend a week or two away. But the industry's continuous use of images of white ships on blue waters carrying gray-haired couples in evening gowns and tuxedos enjoying endless nights of midnight buffets decorated with ice sculptures left a large portion of vacationers questioning cruising as a vacation choice.

Royal Caribbean International, one of the world's largest cruise companies, did research that showed noncruisers perceived cruising to be for three types of travelers: Those newly wed… over fed… or almost dead! If a consumer didn't fit the honeymooner, sedentary, or retired person profile, he or she simply didn't feel that a cruise vacation was a viable option.

Royal Caribbean believed it could change that perception and as a result grow market share. The company decided to turn its cruise line into a breakaway brand by appealing to a different type of vacationer.

Royal Caribbean's research suggested that there was a large untapped audience of individuals who were not in the three typical categories—but were avoiding a cruising vacation because they perceived cruising was only for people in these categories. The new potential audience for cruising was looking for fun, a variety of activities, traveling to different places, new learning, adventure, and excitement. In fact, this is what cruising could offer them… they just didn't perceive that it could.

Royal Caribbean identified their audience as vacation enthusiasts—active adults who look for new experiences and view life as an adventure. These are not sedentary people like the stereotypical cruise passenger—these are individuals who climb rock walls, swim with sting rays, or take unique off-shore excursions.

Royal Caribbean found ways to appeal to this audience. The cruise line was the first to separate its ships from the ordinary ones by building rock-climbing walls and ice skating rinks. Royal Caribbean made sure both on-board and off-board activities were part of a cruising experience geared to these consumers. The advertising message highlighted both ship amenities and destinations so prospective cruise customers would realize they were about to enjoy a multifaceted vacation. For example, a print ad promoting a European cruise (Figure 3-1) features an off-board excursion to the Sistine Chapel, while reminding the consumer that the ship's spa awaits her after a day of sightseeing.

No longer a traditional cruising company, Royal Caribbean became a category of one in the cruising business—a breakaway brand that could attract new customers by widening the definition of what a cruise could be. Now Royal Caribbean could market vibrant vacations that just happened to be cruises to a broader audience.

Royal Caribbean's branding work sets a distinctive tone across every medium the cruising company uses to portray its brand—from television, print, and direct mail, to interactive media, brochures, events, and signage. Using the theme "Get Out There,"

Figure 3-1 Royal Caribbean's print advertising appeals to a more active adult interested in on-board amenities and off-board excursions. This ad promotes cruises to Europe, depicting the ceiling of the Sistine Chapel, along with an appointment card for a massage in the ship's spa. (Image © Vatican Museum & Gallery/Bridgeman Art Library)

Royal Caribbean's look, feel, and message is designed for a different kind of cruising customer. This differentiation has been so unique in the cruising industry that other cruise lines have attempted to copy Royal Caribbean's success.

Royal Caribbean changed the perception of what a cruise could be. The cruise line took a risk by building breakthrough ships that set an industry standard, targeting a specific audience mindset, and developing a breakaway marketing campaign that brought a new view of cruising to the marketplace. Royal Caribbean did this by "turning the lens around." Instead of following all the other cruise lines and featuring the typical ship on the ocean, Royal Caribbean's marketing campaign helps customers see cruising as a rich vacation experience—from on-board excitement and fun to off-board adventure and action.

As a result, Royal Caribbean refocused and grew its business dramatically. From 2000 to 2004, unaided brand awareness increased more than 30 percent; brand preference increased 30 percent; average daily web traffic increased 425 percent; online bookings were up over 300 percent, and loyalty program enrollment was up 90 percent. The average age of Royal Caribbean's first-time cruising customer dropped from 44 years of age in 2000 to 36 years of age in 2004. Royal Caribbean's breakaway strategy paid off.

The Breakaway Brand Creates a Category of One

The breakaway brand stands apart from others in its own category, and often stands out as a model brand that transcends categories. Royal Caribbean in cruises, Starbucks in retail, Dell in computer technology, Miller Lite in beer—these brands each create a "category of one."

The breakaway brand opens a defining gap between itself and its competitors—whether it is new to the market or an existing player. The breakaway brand becomes a category of one—redefining its category so it stands separate and apart from its competitors.

The breakaway brand becomes a category of one—redefining its category so it stands separate and apart from its competitors.

FLYING RIGHT

It is possible to create a category of one even in overcrowded categories such as the airline industry.

With carriers competing for the same routes and a dwindling pool of air travelers, cutting fares has become a way of life. Major carriers with inflated cost structures and a few hubs have gone bankrupt as a result. This has left an opportunity for such carriers as Southwest to provide low-cost no-frills flying.

Southwest was, indeed, the first low-cost carrier to create a category of one. Southwest has achieved significant success by delivering extremely low fares, but it also requires a compromise of sorts: trips originate from secondary airports, seats are unassigned, and frills are nonexistent.

Not everyone who flies wants to give up every convenience for a lower fare, so a feisty start-up called JetBlue created another category of one, differentiating itself from both the majors and Southwest.

JetBlue CEO David Neeleman had sold his first airline, Morris Air, to Southwest Airlines. He learned firsthand how to attract a strong and loyal market. Neeleman started by raising $130 million—more money than any other airline start-up in history. JetBlue acquired the best equipment, hired smart, and could afford to provide the best service.

JetBlue put together a package of industry trendsetting conveniences: paperless tickets, new planes, leather seats, and free satellite TV on every seatback. Then the airline combined these features with low fares based on one-way travel requiring no Saturday night stay. JetBlue backed it all up with impressive on-time performance, superior baggage handling, and excellent customer service.

Even at the outset, the perception of JetBlue was positive—this was an airline that customers and the media held up as a model of what air travel should be. David Neeleman made sure that perception didn't change. With every detail and decision, he reinforced the singularity of JetBlue.

Never veering from its core positioning, JetBlue was profitable within its first year of operation. Two years later, in 2002, JetBlue achieved the highest operating margin of any domestic U.S. airline. Today, with over 18 million customers, the airline continues to expand its fleet and routes even as other airlines scramble to stay aloft.

First Southwest and then JetBlue turned the ailing airline industry upside down. At least two major airlines have launched new brands modeled after JetBlue. Both Song (Delta) and Ted (United) deliberately distanced themselves from their parent carriers. Perhaps the greatest evidence of JetBlue's success, however, was the merger announced by troubled carrier US Airways and America West in May 2005. The new airline will retain the name US Airways. Clearly influenced by the growth of breakaway airlines Southwest and JetBlue, the joint announcement by US Airways and America West said their merger would create "the first nationwide full service low-cost airline."

Like Apple, Nike, and Mercedes-Benz, JetBlue's ascent was based on a strong brand promise. Success truly took off, however, with the passionate, relentless integration of every branding element.

The JetBlue story demonstrates how a breakaway brand has the ability to change the marketplace by creating a category of one. JetBlue saw a gap in a volatile industry that could be filled with the right combination of product, service, and value. By adopting a unique position amongst its competitors, JetBlue achieved early unprecedented success. The company was able to offer value-priced, highly desirable amenities and still become profitable. JetBlue's core positioning remained consistent—and its visionary CEO made sure everything the airline did supported its brand so it would maintain its breakaway status in the marketplace.

DRIVERS WANTED

In a perfect world, you can create a brand new breakaway brand, as did JetBlue. But Volkswagen didn't have that luxury. When the Japanese automakers stole the market away from every other car manufacturer in the mid-1980s, Volkswagen was challenged with a harsh reality: reinvent or become obsolete. Despite the iconic nature of its brand represented by the "Beetle," Volkswagen faced the fact that, suddenly, it was Honda, Toyota, and the other Japanese brands that were breaking away and stealing VW's buyers.

There was a positioning difference, however. Japanese cars were perceived to be tranquil, quiet, and passive. German-made cars were fun, spirited driving machines. You may recall an early ad campaign for Toyota's Avalon that invited consumers to "experience the tranquility." Volkswagen saw the Japanese car experience as not only tranquil, but numbing, kind of like "experiencing the Prozac." To Volkswagen's German engineers, that wasn't what the feeling of driving was all about.

This opened the door for Volkswagen's marketing agency to create a new category of one. Why not make German engineering important again—but in a way that hadn't been done before? Why not separate Volkswagen from both the Japanese and the higher-priced German models such as BMW and Mercedes-Benz?

In 1995, Volkswagen's agency proposed the slogan "Drivers wanted." It was a call to action for drivers, not merely passengers, to wake up and feel the road again. Accompanying ads rebranded Volkswagen as hip, cool, youthful, and fun. VW advertising became known for celebrating the fun of driving—memorable because of its look, music, and slice-of-life stories that focused on the drivers of the cars as much as the cars themselves.

But it wasn't just about the advertising. Volkswagen innovated in its product line as well. It created models of cars built around a youthful mindset, such as the Jetta Trek, a car that came with a mountain bike, and the Golf K2, designed with a roof rack especially for skis and snowboards.

In 1998, Volkswagen continued to separate its brand with a bold move. The company decided to reinvent the widely recognized automobile that was its claim to fame in the first place.

Enter the New Beetle, an updated model of the original, with sassy styling and modern conveniences that could appeal to a broad audience. The redesigned car generated so much buzz, it was featured prominently in a *Business Week* cover story entitled "The Nostalgia Boom."[1] Ads such as the one shown in Figure 3-2, using the headline "Suddenly, the world's glass is half full again," supported the New Beetle launch effort.

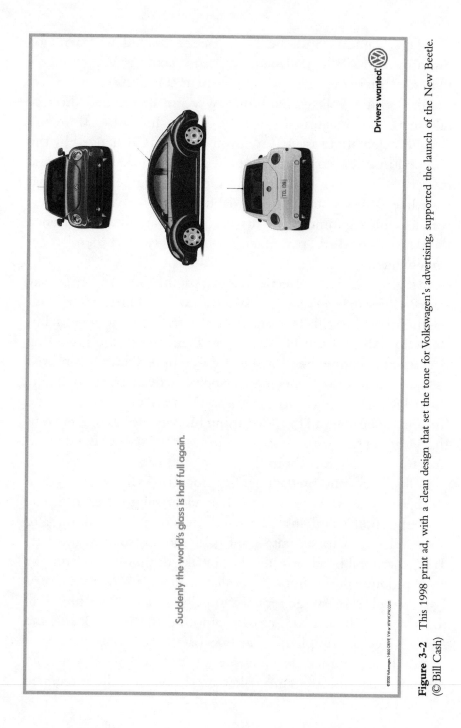

Figure 3-2 This 1998 print ad, with a clean design that set the tone for Volkswagen's advertising, supported the launch of the New Beetle. (© Bill Cash)

"Drivers wanted" and the New Beetle helped fuel a major turnaround for the German car manufacturer: Volkswagen's U.S. sales increased 278 percent from 1994 to 2001.

Like JetBlue, Volkswagen broke away and altered the automobile market by creating a category of one. Instead of throwing away its celebrated past, VW reinvented itself. Challenged by the competition, the company adopted a position that no one else owned. Soon it was cool to drive German-engineered cars that were like BMW's but at an affordable price. Volkswagen discovered its winning mindset in "drivers" who wanted to experience their cars instead of "passengers" who simply used them to get somewhere.

Bringing back the Beetle reinforced the brand's breakaway status. Older drivers reminisced about that odd little car of their youth—the one with the engine in the back that somehow became a symbol of the Flower Power Generation, the Love Bug that starred in movies. But the car was updated and improved so it had true cross-generational appeal. The reinvented Beetle made kids take notice, too, because the new bug was cool and fun and offbeat—and the advertising message was as much about the younger consumer's perception of the New Beetle and Volkswagen as it was about the reinvented car.

Volkswagen innovated with other models in its line to strengthen its appeal to all sorts of drivers. The advertising for each model was aspirational and inspirational. The company continues to do novel things to separate itself. Car models such as the Jetta Trek, memorable advertising that breaks the mold, and unique cross-product promotions have all become part of its strategy. For example, Volkswagen ran a campaign called "Pods unite" in the second half of 2003, cross-promoting the New Beetle and Apple's iPod as complementary two-of-a-kind products.

You'll see numerous mentions of Volkswagen throughout this book because the automaker is a leader in fully integrated marketing campaigns, which typically include traditional and online advertising, web-based promotion, direct mail and e-mail marketing, outdoor, and special events. It is this continuous eye toward innovation that reinforces the exuberance of Volkswagen as a breakaway brand.

NOT YOUR TYPICAL BREAKAWAY BRAND

If ever there were an undifferentiated category, it is banking. Much as banks have tried to break away, most of them are, well, banks. Banks are rarely lauded for being approachable, friendly, and customer-service-oriented.

The leadership of Citizens Bank was determined to change that. Through a series of acquisitions, Citizens had grown from largely a Rhode Island bank in the 1980s to a major force in New England banking and, more recently, a bank of national prominence. With its 2004 acquisition of Charter One Financial, Citizens is now the eighth-largest commercial bank holding company in the United States ranked by deposits.

In 1999 the bank faced a challenging issue that would ultimately define Citizens as a breakaway brand. Citizens Bank CEO Lawrence K. (Larry) Fish explained it this way: "Prospects couldn't fill in the blanks about Citizens."[2] He found that the bank was virtually unknown outside its customer base—and he knew that had to change.

Fish looked for a way to turn Citizens into a category of one. He believed Citizens was a different kind of bank and could make good on that brand promise. His vision was to leverage Citizens as a friendly, warm, approachable bank with employees who were respectful and nice to customers. He believed Citizens was not your typical bank. (In fact, that became Citizens tag line: "Not your typical bank.")

Larry Fish wasn't your typical banker, either. He saw competitors growing larger and more impersonal through acquisition and consolidation, converting systems and customers to a new way of doing things each time. Citizens was making acquisitions too, but according to Fish, the difference was Citizens emphasized integration, not conversion. New employees and converted customers had to feel welcome and at home with their new bank. That was the point at which the bank would be most vulnerable.

With the opening of every new Citizens branch, the bank's biggest worry, says Fish, was "Will we be this nice when we're bigger?" Managing by example, Larry fostered proactive community involvement, offered his employees benefits that touched the heart, and insisted on bank branches that were a pleasure to visit. Citizens even put branches in grocery stores, making banking conveniently available during shopping hours.

The bank's advertising followed suit. Print advertising, such as the ad shown in Figure 3-3, emphasized the friendliness and approachability of Citizens. Billboards, as shown in Figure 3-4, followed the same messaging platform, highlighting the bank's differences from its competition in short, tongue-in-cheek statements.

To powerfully, consistently communicate the brand promise, a series of "legendary service ads" was launched on television, each based on a true story, each with a very human quality. In one spot, a Citizens employee comes out of the branch early in the morning to help a customer make a deposit—only to realize he has locked himself out. In another, a Citizens employee escorts an elderly woman from his supermarket bank branch into the parking lot—only to learn that she has no car and is clearly expecting to be escorted all the way home. These award-winning commercials drive home the bank's strong point of differentiation in a largely undifferentiated category.

Figure 3-3 A Citizens ad simply but powerfully supports the bank's friendly, warm approach with the headline: "Realistically, you may never love your bank. But we're shooting for a long, intense like." (© Ibid, Inc.)

Figure 3-4 Citizens uses this outdoor billboard to reinforce its "not your typical bank" positioning.

The emphasis on friendly service is the very core of the Citizens brand. It has infiltrated every medium, from advertising to brochures to signage—and yes, even those ATM deposit envelopes. It even finds its way into employee training—the bank has launched a motivational program that enlists select bankers in a "friendly corps" to go out into the community and do nice things.

Citizens Bank's "brand truth" banks on both rational and emotional arguments. On the rational side, Citizens is the only bank that offers a unique combination of 24-hour banking, accessibility, convenience, smart products, responsiveness, and customer advocacy. On the emotional side, what Citizens does for the consumer is unexpected in a bank. Citizens is smart, confident, respectful, fair, appreciative, and humanizing.

When Citizens Bank embarked on a new geographic path and launched its brand in the mid-Atlantic region, it adhered to its brand truth consistently. Citizens threw a party for customers, welcoming them with open arms to branches that were warmly lit, cheerful, and friendly—right down to the Hershey's Kisses wrapped in the bank's green color. In Philadelphia, Citizens built a new ballpark for the Philadelphia Phillies. Opened in April 2004, Citizens Bank Park has a separate entrance and a dedicated concession stand for Citizens Bank ATM and debit cardholders.

Breaking away Citizens Bank from the competition is a daily goal for Larry Fish and for every Citizens employee. The Citizens Credo is simple yet compelling: It depends on "living the brand in everything we do for Customers, Colleagues, and the Community." In Larry Fish's words, "Your dedication to the brand goes right to the bottom line."

Getting to the Brand Truth

We've discussed a number of defining characteristics of the breakaway brand: winning positioning, continuous innovation, audience insight, targeting a winning mindset, creating a category of one, relentless integration. These terms, as well as a lot of the marketing mumbo jumbo you hear these days, don't amount to anything unless you recognize that, underneath it all, lies the simple fact that every great brand is built on a truth. Where would Volkswagen, Royal Caribbean, JetBlue, Citizens Bank, Apple, or Mercedes-Benz be without the brand truth that defines and differentiates each of them?

Ultimately, the DNA of a breakaway brand is its brand truth, which can inform every other decision a brand marketer has to make—decisions that prove the brand is authentic and not a fabrication. The brand truth is the single most important weapon a brand will ever have in the battle for increased awareness, profitability, market share, and even share price.

The brand truth is the single most important weapon a brand will ever have in the battle for increased awareness, profitability, market share, and even share price.

Figure 3-5 Company vision, business insights, and target insights help define a winning mindset. All of these elements lead to the brand truth.

To get to the brand truth, every breakaway brand marketing team goes through a process, and top advertising agencies follow a similar process. While each approach varies, the process is essentially the same. This section discusses the basic process we follow to help our clients develop a breakaway brand. Figure 3-5 shows how all of these elements come together in a cohesive form.

COMPANY VISION

A brand is the product of an organization that creates the brand with business goals in mind. Before we can get to the brand truth, it is essential to first understand the company vision—who the company is, what the company's management values are, where they want to go, and what the business challenge is. We find a brand-engaged CEO and a talented, empowered CMO to be MVPs during this first step of the discovery process.

BUSINESS INSIGHTS

To develop business insight, we need to get a comprehensive overview of the brand's category. Business insights include how the company makes money, the characteristics of the competition, what the product is, and where business is going to come from. A truly great branding campaign must be tightly aligned to the key profit-driving elements of the business.

TARGET INSIGHTS

Target insights, in part, involve finding a "cultural wave" that relates to the brand. Catching and riding that wave helps a brand grow cost-effectively. Here we examine cultural trends and do target analysis. We gain insight into how current customers and best prospects use the product, and how the company and product fits within their lives. This is where the communications challenge is defined.

When your brand truly is a little different—a little better than your competition—and that uniqueness truly fits an important need in peoples' lives, you have the foundation of a breakaway brand.

WINNING MINDSET

The company vision, business insights, and target insights combine to help define a winning mindset. The winning mindset is the potent, aspirational, shared "view of life" among a company's best customers *and* its best prospects. It reflects a deep consumer understanding of how best to match the company vision and the product with the target audience. The winning mindset becomes the audience filter through which all advertising and promotional activities flows. If a marketer understands and embraces the winning mindset, the messaging and communications that target the winning mindset can be clearly defined.

Nike revolutionized sports marketing by targeting a super-competitive athletic mindset—not basketball players. Volkswagen broke away in automobiles by targeting and connecting with "drivers." Royal Caribbean's targeting of a different type of cruising customer, someone interested in adventure and excitement, revitalized the entire cruise industry.

BRAND TRUTH

Finally, the moment of truth arrives. The brand's DNA is the brand truth—the ultimate articulation of the brand's most compelling truth that takes into account all previous learning and intersects with our winning mindset's view of life. The brand truth informs all brand behavior. This is, fundamentally, what the brand stands for and represents to the winning mindset.

As indicated earlier, a strong brand truth involves both head and heart. The *rational core* represents the brand aspiration, or what the brand stands for. The *emotional "wrapping"* is the feelings a consumer with the right mindset should have about the brand. Part of the emotional wrapping is the packaging—how the brand appears to the consumer. The brand truth helps us identify and sell the *rational* attributes of a brand in an *emotional* way.

With the rational and emotional come the additional realization that brands live in a highly competitive world; a brand may stand apart, but rarely does it stand alone. The breakaway brand needs to push against something, driving a wedge between itself

The Brand Truth Manifesto

Every great brand is built on a truth. Somewhere beneath the growth charts, beyond the sales forecasts, and beyond the quarterly earnings lies an essential, fundamental, proprietary truth. It's sitting there at the intersection of all things true and all things meaningful. It's what made your current customers your current customers. It's what will draw your best customers to you and even reinforce their own aspirations. It's the truth your employees deliver every day to each other and to your customers. It can make your planning more cohesive, your strategies more powerful, your campaign idea more distinctive, and your communications more unified.

Your brand truth can inform every other decision you have to make—decisions that will prove your brand is authentic and not a fabrication. And in the battle for increased awareness, profitability, market share, and even share price, it is the single most important weapon you will ever have.

and its competitors. The sustainable breakaway brand finds ways to continually widen this gap and become a category of one.

In the end, it's all about getting to the brand truth...and then relentlessly executing that unique brand truth passionately and artfully. It might be a product differentiator (however small), a design advantage, a service commitment, a distribution philosophy, an existing emotional connection people make with a brand, or a combination of many things—some obvious and some not so obvious.

By understanding the brand truth, a brand marketer can create a brand position that turns an ordinary brand into a breakaway brand, and devise a marketing strategy with the power to last well into the future.

Breakaway branders are passionate, brave, and relentless. Most breakaway branding organizations have brand-engaged CEOs and talented, empowered CMOs. Many engage advertising agencies who become valued partners. All of these brand marketers are working toward a common goal—to discover and promote the brand truth that makes their brand stand out from all others.

Chapter 3 Break Points

- THINK ABOUT IT: What are some of the "brand truths" of brands you consider to be breakaway brands? Think about and list your own examples of brand truths, and see how they help separate brands in the marketplace.

- The breakaway brand strives for consistency and sustainability in both its product and its marketing. It begins with a brand marketer targeting a mindset and understanding how to communicate with that mindset—and everything goes through the mindset filter from that point forward.

- The breakaway brand has a strong brand truth. It is the commitment of the brand's owner to the consumer, stated or implied, to make the brand perform as promised.

- The brand truth is both rational and emotional. If the brand truth can embody both the mind *and* the heart and soul, it will be a winning proposition.

- The breakaway brand targets a winning mindset, which articulates the attitude of the brand's best customers and prospects.

- The breakaway brand becomes a category of one—redefining its category so it stands separate and apart from its competitors.

- The DNA of a breakaway brand is its brand truth. To get to the brand truth, every breakaway brand goes through a process.

- Our process for developing a breakaway brand includes company vision, business insight, target insight, winning mindset, and brand truth.

- Breakaway branders are passionate, brave, and relentless.

- Most breakaway branding organizations have brand-engaged CEOs and talented, empowered CMOs.

Breakaway Products

F ewer than 10 percent of all new products or services produce enough ROI to survive past the third year.[1]

This dramatizes the need for breakaway-product development. Breakaway branding can help any product do better in the marketplace. But the only way to build a dominant breakaway brand is to find a way to make your product unique and somehow better.

Breakaway branding can help any product do better in the marketplace. But the only way to build a dominant breakaway brand is to find a way to make your product unique and somehow better.

Breakaway products can be created in any category, but it requires vision, creativity, and guts. It may mean throwing away an old product brand and reinventing it. When its traditional leather Classics brand golf shoes was losing market share, FootJoy invented a new golf shoe called DryJoys. These shoes used a new material called Sympatex that was impervious to water on the outside but allowed the golfer's foot to breathe on the inside. A better product was born, market share went up, and the FootJoy brand was reinvigorated. To this day, FootJoy enjoys a dominant number-1 market share and strong brand loyalty in the golf shoe category.

Alternatively, improving your product may mean starting from scratch. Refrigerated soy milk wasn't even a category before White Wave created Silk, packaged it in colorful milk cartons, and placed it in grocery stores' dairy cases. Now Silk owns the category. The brand rose from zero market share in 1996 to 85 percent in 2003.

A breakaway product could be a first mover in an established category, a product so strong it dominates a category, or the creator of an entirely new category. Regardless, the product itself must have outstanding attributes. It should embody the characteristics we discussed earlier: smart positioning, innovation, an audience connection, leadership, and a strong brand promise. And it must be somehow unique in a way that makes consumers' lives a little better.

Not all breakaway products are successful, and not all successful products are breakaway products. A breakaway product can achieve notoriety in its category but generate weak sales; maybe the product is too expensive or is ahead of its time. A look-alike, me-too product can do reasonably well in a category that is large enough to sustain numerous competitors—but this doesn't mean it is a breakaway product.

When a breakaway product is firing on all cylinders, its success is obvious. The name captures the spirit and persona of the product. The product launch is memorable and creates a lot of buzz. The product stands out in a crowded field—it looks like a winner from the outset and builds momentum. The target audience for the product has positive perceptions; they may even tell others about the product. Even as the product changes and evolves over time, it retains its original aura.

Breaking Away in an Established Category

To break away in an established category, a product must be a first mover or have such unique qualities that it cannot help but stand out. For example, take Nike in athletic footwear (and then sportswear), Starbucks in coffee, and Royal Caribbean in cruising. These products did not establish their respective categories—but each redefined its category.

Nike has become a category of one through its dedication to excellence, innovation, and consistent quality. The Nike product does more than attract customers; it inspires them. Starbucks has reinvented the "coffee house" and makes a gourmet quality product available in a congenial atmosphere, accessible virtually everywhere. Royal Caribbean has created a category of one in cruise vacations, identifying and appealing to an entirely different audience mindset.

Sometimes a breakaway brand in an established category holds its position because it originated the category *and* continues to lead it. Jack Daniel's Tennessee Whiskey is a case in point. Jack Daniel's, the flagship brand of Brown-Forman, is made by America's oldest registered distillery, established in 1866. During the company's Fiscal Year 2004, Jack Daniel's surpassed 7 million cases in global volume; worldwide volumes were up 6 percent during the year. Not only is Jack Daniel's the best-selling American whiskey brand in the world by a wide margin, it is the fifth largest premium spirits brand worldwide.[2]

Let's look at some other examples.

ONE SWEET WORLD

Can a quirky newcomer break away in an established category? Ben & Jerry's proves it—it has the stuff breakaway legends are made of.

In 1978 Ben Cohen and Jerry Greenfield started selling their premium ice cream in a small shop in Burlington, Vermont. By 1984, when Ben & Jerry's came into the Boston, Massachusetts, market, Haagen-Dazs (owned by Pillsbury) made an effort to stop the upstart ice cream company. It was just what Ben & Jerry's needed. The fledgling company filed suit against Pillsbury and launched its notorious publicity campaign, "What's the Dough-boy Afraid Of?" This classic battle of the little independent self-starter pitted against the big corporate giant garnered media and consumer attention alike, and a breakaway brand was born.

From that point on, everything about Ben & Jerry's has been to the left of center. The brand broke a lot of rules and created its own business conventions. It has been true to its Vermont, hippie-esque beginnings, from the iconic founders' "earth father" appearance, to the '60s-style packaging, to the renowned humorous ice cream names, such as Cherry Garcia, Chubby Hubby, Chunky Monkey, Karamel Sutra, and Rain Forest Crunch. From fun has sprung seriously philanthropic pursuits; early on, Ben and Jerry started a foundation to which the company still donates 7.5 percent of its annual pretax profits.

Ben & Jerry's continuous innovation has been one of its brand landmarks. The company has sponsored music festivals in its home state of Vermont and in Newport, Rhode Island, and plays an active role in supporting social and environmental causes. In 1994 the company held a "YO! I'm Your CEO!" contest, inviting candidates for the legitimate position to convince the founders of their worthiness. Over 22,000 people applied for the job.

By the end of 1999, Ben & Jerry's reached worldwide sales of more than $237 million—certainly enough for someone else in the ice cream business to take notice. In 2000 Ben & Jerry's was acquired by Unilever; however, the founders worked a deal that allowed Ben & Jerry's to operate separately from Unilever's U.S. ice cream business, with an independent board of directors to provide leadership for Ben & Jerry's social mission and brand integrity. In 2002 the company reinforced its position as a social do-gooder, launching "One Sweet Whirled," both an ice cream flavor and an environmental action web site designed to help fight global warming.

As a breakaway brand, Ben & Jerry's is a fountain of innovative, fresh ideas. New products such as frozen yogurt and sorbets have been brought to market to keep up with consumer demand, and new flavors introduced annually always bring a smile to the consumer's face. The company runs an annual "Free Cone Day," during which some 450 franchised Ben & Jerry's retail "Scoop Shops" around the world give away free ice cream all day. The April 27, 2004, Free Cone Day was held in collaboration with Rock the Vote in an effort to register new voters across the United States.

MINI-SIZING THE AUTOMOBILE

Breaking away in a crowded category is probably the most difficult of all challenges. In the U.S. auto market, even the subcategories are overpopulated; numerous competitors already own significant market share in compacts, luxury cars, minivans, SUVs, hybrids, and other vehicle classes.

What it takes to break away in this market is an automobile so unlike any other, it doesn't even fit into one of the subcategories.

Enter the MINI.

This tiny car with a transversely mounted engine and room for four adults was launched in Europe in 1959. Small yet safe, economical yet quality-conscious, the MINI became a European sensation by winning major car races. While it was brought to the United States in the 1960s, emission standards introduced in 1968 prevented the MINI from continuing to be sold on American soil. Retreating to its European stronghold, the popularity of the MINI continued to grow, with 5 million cars produced by 1984. In 1994 BMW acquired the MINI, and in 1998 the MINI was listed in the Guinness Book of World Records as the most successful British car in history.

With BMW behind it, a newly designed MINI came to market in 2000. The MINI reentered the U.S. market in 2001, with the MINI Cooper and MINI Cooper S models becoming available by 2002.

MINI breaks away purely because it is the smallest car on U.S. roadways, but that alone doesn't create the momentum a new automobile needs to rise from a fad to a fixture. BMW has continuously innovated with the product, even allowing consumers to "build their own" by offering a wide choice of body- and roof-color combinations. Advances are not purely cosmetic either—the MINI has been so well designed and engineered that it has won numerous awards.

Just as important, MINI breaks away with out-of-the-box, breakthrough marketing created by an agency known for its nontraditional approach, Crispin, Porter + Bogusky. Here are a few examples:

- An outdoor billboard in a desert location shows a MINI with its slogan, "Let's Motor." The billboard is positioned near two simulated palm trees that are bent over, permanently trailing in the MINI's wake.

- A MINI is mounted on the top of a Ford Explorer, painted with the headline, "What are you doing for fun this weekend?" and driven around city streets.

- The MINI is prominently featured in the May 2003 movie, *The Italian Job.* An integral part of the plot, the MINI is seen driving down stairs, speeding through subway tunnels, and navigating sidewalks.

- A wall poster with a picture of the MINI and the headline, "Makes Everything Else Seem a Little Too Big," is placed next to a specially built, oversize pay phone kiosk that actually makes the phone itself appear larger than the MINI.

- An online ad campaign allows consumers to "drive" a MINI, using their keyboards, and interactively "obliterate" a fake web site.

- When U.S. demand for the MINI exceeded supply, BMW created an online program called "Where's My Baby?" to inform anxious owners when to expect delivery. BMW also sent buyers cards and promotional gifts during their waiting period.

According to MINI USA, 10,000 MINIs had been sold in the first 24 weeks after the brand's 2002 U.S. launch. More MINIs were sold in five months than were sold in eight years during the MINI's first U.S. introduction in the 1960s. MINI USA claims that the MINI has created a new subcategory of the American automobile market: the "premium small car."

Breaking Away by Dominating a Category

A breakaway product that dominates a category is the proverbial 600-pound gorilla of the category. While enviable, this position means the product is under continuous attack from competitors who may be happy with the few percentage points of market share they can grab from the acknowledged leader.

Obvious category dominators include the Microsoft Windows operating system for PCs and Wal-Mart, the retailing giant. Despite talk of Linux as an emerging operating system, Windows' dominant market share continues to be untouchable. It contributed directly to Microsoft's nearly $10 billion of profit in 2003. Wal-Mart's revenues of nearly $259 billion in 2003 represented about 2.5 percent of the gross national product (GNP).

Industry estimates indicate that about 50 percent of the American public walks through a Wal-Mart store each week.

It is exceedingly difficult to dominate a category as large as software or retail. Even in smaller categories, however, competition can be intense. The result is that there are few dominators, and even fewer breakaway products. However, our research shows that talented, relentless marketers can build a breakaway brand success in any category. Following are some notable examples.

SETTING THE COURSE IN GOLF

In the venerable world of golf, Titleist and FootJoy are indeed category dominators. These sister brands are number 1 in golf balls and number 1 in golf shoes, respectively.

The first Titleist golf ball was produced in 1935 by the Acushnet Company, a division of Fortune Brands. Acushnet acquired FootJoy in 1985 and formed a golf division, Titleist and FootJoy Worldwide. In the 1990s, the company acquired the Cobra brand. Titleist golf balls have steadily grown to be the overwhelming choice among tour pros and top amateurs. FootJoy has been the number 1 shoe in golf since 1946.

Both brands have continued to be leaders even in the face of a flat golf market and intense competition, most notably from Nike. Nike's Phil Knight reportedly said he wanted to "make Titleist the Converse of golf." Nike's foray into the market was on the coattails of Tiger Woods. In 2000 Woods switched to a Nike-made solid-core golf ball and proceeded to win four Majors in a row.

A major challenge for both Titleist and FootJoy was to neutralize the Tiger Woods factor. From a strategic perspective, Titleist continued to leverage its relationships with many golf pros, recognizing that golf was not just about one player. Titleist and FootJoy used a "pyramid of influence" (see illustration) to represent its various key audiences. At the top of the pyramid were the major tour players. Next were the club pros, nationally ranked amateurs, and collegiate players. The third level was made up of sectional and regional key players, college coaches, and promising juniors. Then came avid golfers (those who played 25 or more rounds per year). Finally, at the bottom of the pyramid were all other golfers.

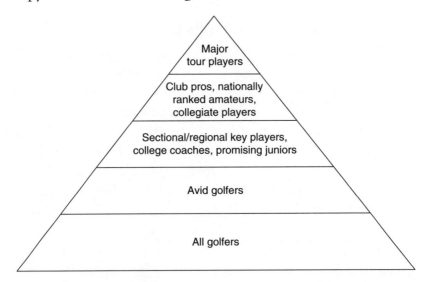

By working hard at reinforcing its position with each of the audiences identified in the pyramid, Titleist targets avid golfers with a very clear message—that Titleist golf balls are the clear choice among the world's best golfers. Titleist then translates this message at the product level, highlighting product performance superiority through winning. The print ad shown in Figure 4-1 is an example of this strategy. Titleist works to maintain brand loyalists while expanding its product line to appeal to different golfer audiences over varying skill levels and handicaps. Finally, Titleist's marketing efforts always include outstanding service

Figure 4-1 This Titleist ad shows some of the best golfers in the world winning tours using the Titleist Pro V1 ball.

and support of the all-important club professionals whose opinions golfers value greatly when they make buying decisions about golf equipment.

From 1998 to 2004, despite Nike's big dollar push into the category, Titleist's market share grew significantly. Their dollar share of the market increased even in the face of a general decline in the golf ball market. Titleist today remains number 1 despite the Nike–Tiger Woods challenge.

FootJoy followed a somewhat parallel path to maintain its leadership position. In 1998 FootJoy was still number 1 but it also faced the challenge of the Nike-Tiger Woods partnership. FootJoy responded with an offbeat advertising campaign in 1999, introducing SignBoy, an over-the-top golf enthusiast who always manages to look silly in front of golf pros. Figure 4-2 shows one of the print ads featuring "SignBoy." In the first three years of the campaign, FootJoy's market share increased, while sales increased over 12 percent. FootJoy again kept a step ahead of Nike when, in 2001, the company relaunched DryJoys shoes and created a new line of outerwear. As a result, outerwear sales grew 259 percent from 1999 to 2001, and DryJoys became the number-1 all-weather performance brand in golf.

Titleist and FootJoy have withstood competitive challenges from Nike as well as other brands, and they have remained breakaway brands as well as category leaders. Despite a slow-growth golf market, Titleist and FootJoy have become the leading brands of the Achusnet Company, golf's first and only billion dollar business. Along the way, each brand launched new, innovative products and created new advertising campaigns—while never compromising product quality or abandoning core audiences.

ALL THE WORLD'S AN E-MARKET

In the online world, category dominators are few and far between. Amazon.com has withstood the test of time to become the Internet's leading retailer. Google has risen to become the

Figure 4-2 Advertising for FootJoy features SignBoy, an over-the-top golf enthusiast. (© 2003 Jimmy Williams; all player images © Getty Images)

top search-engine, filing a much-anticipated IPO in August 2004 and building significant value along the way. By mid-2005, Google's stock price was three times that of its initial offering. Already an Internet-based giant, Google is now viewed by industry analysts as a major competitor to the dominant player in computer software, Microsoft. But there is another company that has broken away by both creating *and* dominating an Internet category: eBay. eBay, the online auction service, has been a breakaway brand since its inception in 1995. Founder Pierre Omidyar launched eBay as a hobby, pioneering the auction format for online person-to-person trading. He created a simple, easy-to-understand mechanism that lets buyers and sellers decide the true value of items and connect with others.

Some consider it the largest flea market in the world, but today eBay calls itself "The World's Online Marketplace." By the end of March 2005, eBay had over 147 million registered users from more than 150 countries, a 40 percent increase over the prior year. In the first quarter (Q1) of 2005 alone, item listings by users totaled a record 431.8 million, according to the company. The total value of all successfully closed listings on eBay (Gross Merchandise Volume) in Q1 2005 was $10.6 billion, an increase of 32 percent from Q1 2004. Consolidated net revenues reached a record $1.032 billion for Q1 2005, an increase of 36 percent from Q1 2004. It took eight years for eBay to reach $1 billion in annual revenue; however, the company reached that amount in the first three months of 2005 alone.

These are very big numbers. Indeed, eBay is responsible for a kind of online mini-economy. Thousands of small businesses have created a cottage industry by functioning as full- or part-time sellers on eBay. Offshoot businesses servicing the eBay economy have popped up as well—there are now firms that specialize in packaging and shipping especially for eBay sellers.

Despite its growth from a small folksy trading place to an online leader, what turned eBay into a breakaway brand in the first place still resides in the company's DNA. eBay remains committed to community and continues to promote one-to-one communication among all users. eBay offers active discussion boards and chat, a personalized "My eBay" page that tracks a user's buying and selling activity, and its industry-leading "Feedback Forum," where registered users can leave positive or negative feedback on other users based on their buying and selling experiences. This self-policing rating system keeps the community informed and weeds out unscrupulous users.

eBay sells nothing tangible. It is completely a transactional service business that earns its revenue from the actions of others. You might say that eBay is the world's largest commercial e-broker.

There have been and continue to be other online auction marketplaces. Even Amazon has introduced its own variant, allowing customers to sell used books on its site. But no online marketplace has ever approached the massive size, committed user base, or financial success of eBay.

Breaking Away by Creating a Category

A breakaway product that creates a category exerts extraordinary power in that category, often for a long time. eBay's sustainable position as the undisputed leader now makes it difficult if not impossible for a competitor to match its superiority. eBay will always own the perception in the mind of the consumer as the first online auction service.

New categories create new breakaway opportunities. Take Vonage, for example. Founded in January 2001, Vonage quickly took the leadership position in an emerging technology category: broadband telephone service, or "Voice over IP" (VoIP). Using a consumer's existing cable or DSL broadband service and touch-tone telephone, Vonage offers low-cost telephone service over the Internet as an alternative to traditional telephone service. The very nature of the product is redefining the telecommunications industry. The fastest growing telephony company in North America, Vonage ended 2004 with more than 390,000 lines in service, having added 115,000 lines in Q4 alone. According to the company, by March 2005, Vonage had exceeded 500,000 total lines in service on its network, doubling its growth rate—up 50 percent from the fourth quarter of 2004. In 2005, Vonage was reportedly adding about 15,000 lines per week.

Vonage challenged conventional marketing wisdom when it launched its brand. Many new brands turn to television's broad reach for a product launch, but Vonage chose instead to rely heavily on online advertising. By investing online, Vonage could reach its target audience of early adopters who had broadband, with a direct, cost-effective, and measurable approach. It was only after this initial successful campaign built momentum that Vonage started running television commercials in early 2005. These spots highlighted the company's low-price proposition, showing such mishaps as a boy accidentally smashing a window with a baseball bat, accompanied by the headline: "People do stupid things. Like pay too much for phone service."

The breakaway product that creates a category can become so closely associated with its category that the two are inseparable. Earlier we mentioned such examples as Coca-Cola in soft drinks, Federal Express in overnight delivery, and Kleenex in tissues. Each of these brands is still inextricably associated with its respective category today, despite the entry of many competitors.

Here are some additional examples of breakaway category creators.

MILKING THE MILK MARKET

This is the story of a product that created a new category within a category. In the consumer's mind, milk is a seemingly simple established category. Several subcategories have emerged in recent years: skim milk, two-percent low-fat milk, flavored milk, and so on.

There is another subcategory within the milk market: milk substitutes. Cow's milk is not for everyone. Lactose-intolerant individuals cannot drink it, and some people don't like its taste. This gave rise to a category of milk substitute products, one of which was soy milk.

Soy milk was an oddity. Sold primarily in health stores, soy milk was aseptic—packaged via a high-heat process so it could be stored in square-shaped packages on the grocery shelf rather than in the dairy case. This extended the shelf life of soy milk indefinitely, but it contributed to a slightly nutty flavor. It also contributed to a sales challenge: Since the soy milk was stocked on shelves and not next to refrigerated milk, consumers didn't see it as an alternative to cow's milk.

A company called White Wave had the idea to create a new category: refrigerated soy milk. It named its product Silk. In order to position Silk against "real" milk, the product needed to be in the dairy case, right next to the milk.

It was 1996, and no one had ever sold refrigerated soy milk on a national basis. White Wave innovated by creating a dry soy mixture and shipping it off to dairies—the same dairies that processed cow's milk. The dairies added water, packaged the product in Silk's milk look-alike containers, and distributed it, much as if it were refrigerated cow's milk. The dairies were happy to cooperate—they were using downtime in their processing plants to create an additional revenue stream.

White Wave had figured out the first part of the challenge—how to break Silk away from all the other soy milks. Now the company's challenge was to "unseparate" Silk in the mind of the consumer, so that it was viewed as a true cow's milk alternative.

There was no doubt that soy milk simply isn't the same as cow's milk. That's why White Wave decided to first market Silk through natural foods stores, where consumers were likely to be more receptive to it. Yet there was still a large, untapped market for soy milk in the traditional grocery store. What about the audience who weren't necessarily "health nuts"—people who were lactose-intolerant, people who wanted to lower their cholesterol, and people who wanted another source of protein in their diets? These consumers were White Wave's ultimate market for Silk.

White Wave's big break came in October 1999, when the FDA announced that soy was considered a heart-healthy substance that could lower cholesterol. This provided the company with a springboard that legitimized soy milk as a mainstream product. Now White Wave could make the claim that soy milk on your cereal was an easy, simple way to get more soy into your diet. White Wave used the announcement as the basis for a publicity campaign, but they had little money to spend on advertising. Instead, White Wave employed guerilla marketing.

A major challenge was getting consumers to try the product. White Wave decided to rely on aggressive store sampling. To keep the sampling nonconfrontational, Silk was packaged in half-pints, like the little milk cartons kids get at school. Then these samples were offered free, along with coupons, to shoppers on their way out of grocery stores. This way, mom and dad could try the product at home, with no pressure, and decide if it was right for them and their children. The FDA approval appeared prominently on the packaging to reinforce the purchase decision. White Wave also distributed free samples at worthy events, such as Race for the Cure, where health-conscious consumers would congregate.

It was just as important to get traditional grocers to stock Silk in their dairy cases. White Wave again used the third-party endorsement of the FDA to its advantage. It pointed out to grocery chains that soy milk was an increasingly popular product in health food stores. White Wave knew it had to sell at least a case of Silk a week to keep the grocers happy. The company guaranteed to remove the product if it did not sell.

White Wave used its modest promotional budget wisely. The company invested in lush full-color photography of the soy milk flowing against brightly colored backgrounds. The packaging itself carried interesting facts about soy as well as other educational and amusing copy. The company also showed its quirky environmental consciousness by promoting windmill-driven energy on its cartons. The objective was to keep that soy milk carton sitting on the kitchen table as long as possible. The company purchased outdoor billboards and signage on buses in select cities where Silk's distribution was strong. This was accompanied by sponsorships on National Public Radio. The feeling was that NPR listeners fit the Silk drinker's profile. If the consumer was listening to NPR on his or her morning or afternoon drive, and saw Silk riding by on the side of a bus, the media buy would pay off.

White Wave employed a clever tactic to make Silk look more popular than it actually was. The company purchased truck sides and plastered them with bright bold photos of the Silk soy milk containers, as shown in Figure 4-3. Consumers in select markets started to see Silk trucks riding down Main Street. The only thing is, a lot of those trucks didn't contain Silk soy milk at

Figure 4-3 This truck appears to be carrying Silk soy milk—but actually, White Wave just bought the space on the side of the truck so it would look like its product was popular in select markets.

all—they contained other products. White Wave had just bought the space on the trucks to make a lasting impression.

With these types of marketing tactics, Silk soy milk became a category of one. Silk went from having zero share in the soy milk market in 1996 to 85 percent in 2003. The chocolate-flavored Silk became a kind of "good for you" adult chocolate milk and rose to the position of number-2 chocolate milk brand in the country. Chances are good that today you'll find Silk soy milk in your grocer's dairy case…right next to the cow's milk.

Not surprisingly, White Wave's success didn't go unnoticed by potential buyers. In 2001 Dean Foods Co. acquired White Wave. At first, White Wave founder Steve Demos didn't welcome the acquisition. Demos worried that Dean would "damage his company's culture."[3] But the deal went through, and Dean bought the company for $154 million. *The Wall Street Journal* reported that sales for Silk soy milk were projected to reach $414 million in 2005.

While other competitors have entered the refrigerated soy milk category, White Wave isn't waiting for them to catch up. For example, the company worked out a partnership deal for Silk to become the exclusive soy milk used by Starbucks. With this kind of category-leading momentum, competitors have yet to rival Silk's supremacy.

THE iTUNES IDEA

Earlier we discussed Apple's introduction of the iPod, a breakaway digital music player that brought the company headlong into the consumer electronics world. While other players existed when iPod entered the market in late 2001, a case can be made that this breakaway product did indeed create a new category.

iPod was one of the only players at the time to feature a hard disk, and it revolutionized the category with its small size and capacity. One of its most compelling advantages was the iTunes connection. iTunes arrived in the marketplace at a time when the controversy around free (and illegal) music downloads was reaching its high point. iTunes capitalized by offering a reasonably priced download library, fueling the sale of iPods and positioning Apple as the music industry's hero.

Still, the iPod was a Macintosh-only device until 2002, when Apple introduced a PC version. This, coupled with the launch of the iTunes Music Store in 2003, created an unbeatable combination—industry-leading digital music player technology plus the largest legal library of songs available.

iPod broke away as much because of its generational appeal as its technology. Apple clearly had a picture of its target audience and plugged into a deep emotional and lifestyle connection. Teens and young adults carried their music everywhere, but typically they had to carry their CDs along too. Through innovation and smart marketing, Apple made music portable in a way that was easy, convenient, and legal.

By fall 2003, Apple had sold 13 million iTunes songs, and by January 2004, Apple had sold 2 million iPods. The Yankee Group, a research firm, said iPod's U.S. market share in mid-2004 was as much as 60 percent. Perhaps iPod is on the way to becoming American youth's other portable electronic necessity, second only to the cell phone. In early 2005, Apple rocked the market once again with the introduction of a $99 iPod.

IT STARTED AS A JOKE

A final example of a breakaway brand that created a category is a company its founder says "started as a joke and got out of control." That's how actor Paul Newman describes Newman's Own, a company so unique it is hard to categorize at all.

Newman and friend A. E. Hotchner enjoyed bottling home-made salad dressing and giving it as gifts to friends and neighbors for the holidays. Everyone loved it, so the pair was inspired to market the product. In 1982, Newman's Own began selling a single product, Oil & Vinegar Salad Dressing.

There were plenty of salad dressings on the market, so how did Newman's Own break away and create a category of one? This was the only salad dressing company that gave away all of its profits, after taxes, to educational and charitable organizations. The motto of the company is "Shameless Exploitation in Pursuit of the Common Good."

One thing led to another, and today Newman's Own offers a broad range of food products—salad dressings, pasta sauces, salsa, popcorn, lemonade, steak sauce, cookies, and more—in the U.S. and worldwide. The company isn't afraid to innovate,

either: In March 2003, Newman's Own and McDonald's announced an unusual alliance that made Newman's Own the
exclusive supplier of all-natural salad dressings for McDonald's
Premium Salads.

Personality is very much a part of the Newman's Own breakaway formula. Each product carries an artist's rendering of Paul
Newman. Few products make such obvious use of celebrity
endorsement. It is Newman's likeness and his status as a superstar actor that break the company and its products away from
any others. Newman's pledge to donate profits to charity only
enhances the image of the enterprise. This is a brand promise
that can't be beat. Why wouldn't the consumer show a brand
preference for Newman's Own when she knows that buying
the product is also doing good?

Through Paul Newman's efforts, over $150 million has been
donated to thousands of charities since 1982—which only goes
to prove that you don't need to keep your profits to be a breakaway company.

All of these examples share common traits: Breakaway brands
never rest. Breakaway branders never stop driving their brands
ahead. As a result, breakaway brands often generate sustained
sales growth, higher margins, stronger customer loyalty, and
higher profits.

Chapter 4 Break Points

- THINK ABOUT IT: In addition to the breakaway products mentioned in this chapter, consider others that have
  shaken up their respective categories: Altoids mints in a
  tin; Friexenet champagne in a black bottle; Smartfoods
  popcorn in a black bag; the breakaway design of the
  iMac; Amtrak's bullet-like Acela train; Trivial Pursuit, the

breakaway game now in its 20th Anniversary Edition. Make your own list of breakaway products—those you think have created or re-created categories and revolutionized the product world. What strategies have these products used to break away?

- Breakaway products can be created in any category, but it requires vision, creativity, and guts.

- Fewer than 10 percent of all new products or services produce enough ROI to survive past the third year.

- Nothing is more important in building a breakaway brand than creating a unique, better product.

- To break away in an established category, a product must be a first mover or must utilize its own unique qualities to somehow create a category of one.

- A breakaway product that dominates a category is enviable, but this position means the product is under continuous attack from competitors who may be happy with the few percentage points of market share they can grab from the acknowledged leader.

- Breakaway brands never rest. Breakaway branders never stop driving their brands ahead.

- Breakaway brands often generate sustained sales growth, higher margins, stronger customer loyalty, and higher profits.

CHAPTER 5

Breakaway Campaigns

"Just do it." "Think Different." "Drivers wanted." "The #1 ball in golf." "A Diamond Is Forever." "got milk?" "Priceless."

Breakaway products become breakaway brands because of breakaway branding campaigns. Without a strong campaign, a breakaway product can fail and a breakaway brand can fade away.

For a new brand, a campaign is its introduction to the public. For an existing brand, a campaign can increase interest and drive up sales and profits. For a declining brand, the right campaign can renew consumer interest and rejuvenate sales.

A campaign is a large undertaking that could involve millions of dollars of investment in an intricate program of integrated advertising and promotional strategies and tactics. Every element of a breakaway campaign is carefully orchestrated to play off the other, and each element must ultimately support the brand and the brand promise.

The breakaway campaign is a defining moment for a new brand, because the campaign can literally make or break the brand. It is at once the most likely place for success and failure—high risk for high reward. Developing breakaway campaigns takes brains. It is part science; but it is also part art—the great campaigns involve vision, creativity, and passion as well.

A breakaway campaign stands out in the crowd because it cuts through the clutter, connects with the consumer, differentiates the brand from all of its competitors—*and it sells*. It can be for any product in any market. The breakaway campaign is one that "has legs" and can live beyond the initial launch. It not only brings a breakaway brand to market, it also sustains that brand by evolving over time. While the tactics may change, the underlying strategy and message of a breakaway campaign often remains for many, many years.

A breakaway campaign stands out in the crowd because it cuts through the clutter, connects with the consumer, differentiates the brand from all of its competitors—and it sells.

Apple's "Think Different" campaign led to the company's turnaround, creating a different perception about the computer maker that had a lasting impact on the consumer. Miller Lite's "Tastes Great. Less Filling." campaign not only launched a new brand, it launched a whole new beer category, causing competitors to scramble to introduce light beers. Volkswagen's "Drivers wanted" campaign redefined automobile advertising with a human, endearing element—so reinvigorating the brand that VWs became the coolest cars to drive.

Nike's "Just do it" campaign defined not just a brand, but a lifestyle. While the tag line and the ubiquitous "swoosh" are the world's most recognized advertising elements, it is Nike's relentless application of these elements to everything it does that makes the company a legendary marketer. Nike's overarching campaign isn't about athletic shoes, it is about the achievement and performance of athletes. In sport after sport, Nike has applied the "Just do it" magic to achieve breakaway status. While competitors like Reebok have marketed sneakers, Nike has marketed mindset.

Even when Nike gets involved in philanthropic campaigns, something special happens. Nike committed $1 million to the "Live Strong" cancer education program of the Lance Armstrong Foundation to jumpstart the sale of yellow wristbands with the words LIVE STRONG on them. Each wristband would sell for $1, with every dollar going directly to cancer research. The wristbands quickly became hot properties, in part because of Nike's support—worn by athletes and celebrities, and sold on eBay. While the goal was to sell 5 million wristbands, 15 million of them had been sold by the fall of 2004.

Breakaway campaigns like Nike's, Apple's, and Volkswagen's have something else in common: teamwork. Great campaigns are a team sport—they require a partnership between a brand owner, all of its divisions, and its agency to create great campaigns. Just as important, it takes a CMO and CEO with the vision, guts, and determination to take risks, to innovate instead of imitate, and to demand that their organization and advertising agency deliver a breakaway campaign.

Great campaigns are a team sport—they require a partnership between a brand owner, all of its divisions, and its agency to create great campaigns.

It's Magic

Look at a memorable breakaway campaign and you sometimes wonder, "How did they come up with that?" Companies and their agencies alike will tell you a lot goes into a campaign— naming the product, consumer research, smart media buys, flawless execution. But there's a certain amount of magic in there too. At some point, a team of creative people thinks up the ideas that bring a campaign to life. The hard part isn't coming up with lots of creative concepts—many agencies are quite capable of throwing ideas up on a wall. The real magic is *picking the right one*—the big idea that really works, the breakaway concept that becomes the driving force behind a breakaway campaign.

It's how Michelin decided to sit babies in their tires to dramatize safety. It's how Altoids used packaging to differentiate breath mints from all others on the market. It's how ABSO-LUT turned the shape of its bottle into the centerpiece of a breakaway promotional strategy. It's how AFLAC used a quacking duck to create brand awareness, which has increased from about 10 percent to 90 percent since the duck first appeared in January 2000. It's how Volkswagen turned "Drivers wanted" into the most recognizable phrase in automotive advertising. It's how Citizens Bank became known as "not your typical bank" by being friendly and approachable. It's how Royal Caribbean changed cruises into exciting vacation experiences. It's how marketers of Las Vegas thought to tell the world, "What Happens Here Stays Here."

The Campaign Is the Core

A campaign uses a combination of coordinated, integrated media to capture the personality of the product, generate awareness among the right target audiences, and create demand. Past campaigns almost always relied heavily on network television, but modern campaigns are much more varied. Today, campaigns incorporate both network and cable TV, as well as print, online, radio, direct mail, and often nontraditional media—everything from street marketing to publicity stunts to contests that may appear on the product packaging itself.

Marketers and their advertising partners talk about brands that "buzz." Great campaigns go beyond the rational to touch peoples' lives and generate interest and excitement.

The core campaign is the filter for all promotional activities surrounding the brand. Developing a breakaway campaign is easy to talk about but hard to do. The breakaway campaign has the potential to catapult a brand into the culture, create an aspirational connection, and endure for many years. Following are a few classic breakaway campaigns.

The breakaway campaign has the potential to catapult a brand into the culture, create an aspirational connection, and endure for many years.

GOT MILK?

The California Milk Processor Board (CMPB), established in 1993 to "make milk more competitive and increase milk consumption in California," is behind the wildly successful "got milk?" campaign, credited with injecting new life into the U.S. dairy industry.

Conceived by the ad agency Goodby, Silverstein & Partners, the tag line, "got milk?" was introduced in a television ad that ran in October 1993. The ad featured an American history buff who is eating a peanut butter sandwich and tries to answer a radio station's trivia question, "Who shot Alexander Hamilton?" to win $10,000. He knows the answer is Aaron Burr, but he is unable to enunciate the words because his mouth is full of peanut butter...and he has run out of milk, so he can't wash it down. The ad ends with the now classic line, "got milk?" This ad swept the advertising industry's most prestigious awards and was named one of the top ads of all time in numerous polls.

This was the beginning of a breakaway campaign that changed the American public's perception of milk. It was a campaign not without risk. Every previous message about milk conveyed how good it was for you and how it built strong bones. This may have been accurate, but it was dull, dull, dull. Many beverages had passed milk by. "got milk?" recognized not the classic health benefits but rather the contemporary "benefits" of milk. Milk became relevant again, because it was the perfect companion beverage to junk food like peanut butter, cookies, and chocolate cake.

In 1995 CMPB licensed the "got milk?" trademark nationally and the rest, as they say, is history. Other "got milk?" ads won major ad awards in 1994, 1996, 1997, and 2003. Print ads showing celebrities with "milk mustaches" became a national sensation.

By the late '90s, "got milk?" became so ingrained into American culture that countless takeoffs ("got wine?", "got catnip?", etc.) turned the celebrated tag line into a pop culture icon.

In 2004 Great Britain's Milk Development Council licensed "got milk?" to begin a promotion for dairy farmers in the UK—the first time the American campaign had gone international. Meanwhile, back in the U.S., "got milk?" has been licensed on a variety of consumer goods, including t-shirts and other apparel, kitchenware, Hot Wheels, and Barbie dolls. And the "got milk?" slogan has been paired with such cookie manufacturers as Keebler and Nabisco to advertise cookies and milk together.

"got milk?" has achieved over 90 percent awareness nationally.

According to CMPB, "got milk?" has achieved over 90 percent awareness nationally. It has single-handedly revitalized a moribund industry after a 20-year sales slump.

A DIAMOND IS FOREVER

Perhaps more historic than "got milk?" as an industry-changing tag line is "A Diamond Is Forever." Created by the ad agency N.W. Ayer, the tag line itself was written in 1948, but the campaign started in earnest in 1939 as part of a concerted effort by the De Beers diamond cartel to market and sell more expensive diamonds.

In his book *The Diamond Invention* (Arrow/Random House, 1982), Edward Jay Epstein exhaustively details the story of how De Beers created demand in the United States for larger, more expensive diamonds through a carefully orchestrated advertising and publicity campaign. In 1939 diamond prices had collapsed in a Europe that was approaching war. In the United States, the diamond engagement ring was already an American tradition, but the size and quality of the diamonds being presented left much to be desired—at least in the opinion of De Beers.

The Ayer advertising agency studied the market and determined that the way to sell larger, higher quality—and, therefore, more expensive—diamonds was to embark on a broad campaign designed to create societal change. Epstein located Ayer documents from the original campaign that addressed the challenge:

> Specifically, the Ayer study stressed the need to vitalize the association in the public's mind between diamonds and romance. Since "young men buy over 90% of all engagement rings," it would be crucial to inculcate in them the idea that diamonds were a gift of love: the larger and finer the diamond, the greater the expression of love. Similarly, young women had to be encouraged to view diamonds as an integral part of any romantic courtship.[1]

Ayer devised a strategy that was the forerunner of today's "advertainment"—using entertainment as a primary vehicle for product promotion. The agency suggested that diamond engagement rings become a featured attraction in motion pictures; in fact, Ayer said, they wanted to arrange for scenes to be written into movies being produced at the time. Because movie stars represented romantic figures, their fictional presentation of diamond rings as symbols of lasting love would undoubtedly influence mass audiences.

Ayer took the strategy further than movies alone, placing stories and society photographs about diamonds, creating extravagant ads in elite magazines, and even enlisting Queen Elizabeth to promote the royalty of diamonds.

By 1948, when the copy line "A Diamond Is Forever" appeared, Ayer's campaign had already helped increase the sale of diamonds in the U.S. by 55 percent. The agency and De Beers continued to innovate. Ayer used the successful movie-placement strategy to again influence programming, this time in the new medium—television. The agency also created a "Diamond Information Bureau"—in essence, a self-serving publicity arm distributing volumes of material about diamonds that wound up in newspapers and magazines.

By 1948, when the copy line "A Diamond Is Forever" appeared, Ayer's campaign had already helped increase the sale of diamonds in the U.S. by 55 percent.

Today, "A Diamond Is Forever" lives on as the official slogan of the "Diamond Trading Company," the De Beers Group's marketing arm. De Beers calls its tag line the "forevermark."[2] The slogan is still the basis for contemporary campaigns that extol the virtues of diamond engagement rings.

According to Edward Jay Epstein, it was this breakaway campaign strategy originally conceived by N.W. Ayer in 1939 that helped increase De Beers' diamond sales from $23 million in 1939 to over $2 billion at the wholesale level by 1980. This was on an advertising investment that scaled from $200,000 a year initially to $10 million annually. "A Diamond Is Forever" remains an enduring symbol of how an advertising message can have an extraordinary impact on the value people place on an object—and how that value can reflect society's values.

PRICELESS

MasterCard's "Priceless" campaign is so ubiquitous that the copywriting style has become an intentionally imitated format. *The New York Times* advertising columnist Stuart Elliott mimicked the advertising:

> *Annual spending by MasterCard to advertise in major media: about $300 million.*
>
> *Portion of that spending earmarked for advertisements in magazines and newspapers: about 15 percent to 20 percent of the total.*
>
> *Having a print campaign that not only stands out from other ads in magazines and newspapers but is also distinct from the MasterCard television commercials: priceless.*[3]

This unique copy style has been the basis for a campaign with the theme, "There are some things money can't buy. For everything else, there's MasterCard." But it is the word "priceless" that immediately caught on and has become part of the American vernacular. As with "got milk?", the slogan "Priceless" has been often repeated, adapted, and even parodied.

Until recently, MasterCard and Visa have owned the bank credit card market.[4] To the consumer, the brands MasterCard and Visa may appear to be interchangeable, given their subordinate position to the issuing bank. These two brands remained largely undifferentiated until each began major advertising campaigns of their own.

Visa's promotional campaign, "It's everywhere you want to be," was launched in 1985. This campaign has largely positioned the Visa brand against archrival American Express, not Master-Card; in recent years, Visa has pointedly referenced establishments that "don't take American Express."

On the other hand, MasterCard's "Priceless" campaign, created by McCann Erickson and launched in October 1997, had a different objective. Emphasizing the consumer credit utility of the credit card, the "Priceless" campaign adds an emotional element to the purchasing process. The campaign makes the point that the cost of certain items is one thing, but the emotional value of those items is quite another. It may be a special moment with a grandchild, or it may just be something that makes life a little easier; whatever they are, these "priceless" things have undoubtedly raised brand awareness for MasterCard.

Seen in 96 countries and in 47 languages, the "Priceless" campaign has earned more than 100 individual advertising awards. MasterCard says "Priceless" has been heralded as one of the most successful campaigns ever created.

Seen in 96 countries and in 47 languages, the "Priceless" campaign has earned more than 100 individual advertising awards.

Beyond the Launch

Notable among the breakaway campaigns cited above is an all-too-rare characteristic: longevity. Breakaway campaigns become legendary when they contain a core idea so true and executions so fresh that they sustain and actually improve over the years. Yet many brand marketers tire of a campaign long before it has run its course. Agencies and advertisers alike fall prey to changing a campaign before they need to—and the result is a new approach that may disregard or, worse, contradict the original campaign.

Breakaway campaigns become legendary when they contain a core idea so true and executions so fresh that they sustain and actually improve over many years.

The breakaway campaign should be designed to last for five years or more. This doesn't mean it becomes trite or boring; rather, it evolves to a new place. "got milk?" stays fresh by reinventing itself with variations on the theme, as in a series of ads that shows a number of creative and amusing ways to shake up a bottle of chocolate milk. The tag line, "got chocolate milk?" is a smart way to extend the campaign without deadening the original's quirky appeal. At the same time, it promotes a product (chocolate milk) that is an extension of the brand itself (milk).

"A Diamond Is Forever" continues to be as relevant now as it was over forty years ago. The love story has been modernized: In one ad, a man is shown proclaiming his love for a woman by first shouting it at a public square, and then presenting her with a diamond anniversary ring. The messaging about the quality of the diamond is no less prominent in the contemporary television and print advertising that still appears today.

MasterCard's "Priceless" campaign could have stopped at promoting the brand image. Instead the company took the campaign to the next level. In 2004 MasterCard began to reference other retail product brands that can be purchased with a MasterCard credit card. The extension of the original campaign is a win–win: MasterCard continues to ram home its brand message while associating itself with brand names familiar to the consumer. Those brands become direct beneficiaries of the MasterCard campaign.

Keeping a campaign fresh and vibrant—and maintaining its breakaway status—is a major challenge. The competitive landscape is turbulent and consumer perceptions are constantly shifting. It takes courage and perseverance to sustain a breakaway campaign.

THAT'S THE TRUTH

An example of just such an effort is the highly successful yet controversial "truth" campaign. Created by the American Legacy Foundation,[5] truth is a first-of-its-kind national youth antismoking effort. The campaign's goal was to "outbrand" Big Tobacco and create an antismoking brand for teens that would be cooler than smoking. Arnold Worldwide and a close partner agency, Crispin Porter + Bogusky, were selected in 1999 to launch the truth brand.

For truth to work, the teen audience had to be researched, studied, and understood. Teens who were most open to smoking were found to have a common mindset, defined as "sensation seekers." These teens liked new experiences, breaking rules, and doing risky and dangerous things. Such behaviors are all about control. Smoking cigarettes is an ideal way for the sensation seeker to take control. It's a way to look rebellious, fit in, take a risk, be cool.

truth had to fulfill these same needs to achieve success. To compete with the tobacco companies, truth's countermarketing efforts had to be more aspirational and more rebellious than smoking itself.

truth did that by challenging the tobacco industry and demystifying smoking. The breakaway truth campaign simply but powerfully tells the truth about the industry, their products, their marketing and manufacturing practices, and, ultimately, the consequences of it all. In so doing, truth inspires teens to rethink their perceptions about smoking and cigarettes. The campaign also took teens' need to rebel and directed this rebellion at the tobacco industry, allowing teens to turn away from cigarettes in the process.

To compete with the tobacco companies, truth's countermarketing efforts had to be more aspirational and more rebellious than smoking.

Sustaining the campaign has been nothing short of exhausting because of the ever-changing interests of teens. truth strives to modify its delivery of the message by looking for fresh, innovative, edgy ways to talk to teens. truth is always striving for new ways to break through and surprise its target audience in unconventional ways. While the delivery may change over the life of the campaign, the core creative platform is always grounded in truth's brand truth—dispensing honest facts and information that exposes Big Tobacco, but wrapping them in rebellious, risky, empowering, independent, and intelligent emotion.

truth relies on a strategy that calls for an overall campaign with many subthemes. Each mini-campaign typically lasts no longer than six months. Regardless of the theme, numerous teen-appropriate media are used; television, radio, a web site, online and mobile advertising, promotional events and tours, and truth merchandise are tightly integrated for maximum impact.

One truth campaign centered around the fact that the tobacco industry gets away with murder. A television ad used body bags to shock teens into awareness. Another ad showed 1,200 teens falling to the ground outside a tobacco company's headquarters. One teen holds up a sign that reads, "Tobacco kills 1,200 people a day." Another teen holds up a sign that reads, "Ever think about taking a day off?" This ad, a frame of which is shown in Figure 5-1, won numerous industry awards, but more importantly, research shows that teens notice and talk about each new truth television spot.

Another truth campaign featured Crazyworld, a mythical amusement park. One television ad shows a carnival barker leading contestants through "The Ingredient Game." Dripping with sarcasm, the object of the game is to find any product without a list of ingredients. Only a pack of cigarettes wins. The campaign was augmented with a Crazyworld web site, complete with interactive carnival games.

Figure 5-1   This frame from an award-winning television ad for the truth campaign shows a teen holding up a sign in front of a tobacco company's headquarters.

During the 2004 Super Bowl, truth launched a bold campaign called "Shards o' Glass." A television ad introduced viewers to "Shards o' Glass Freeze Pops," a spoof product the supposed company CEO admitted was dangerous and "for adults only." The commercial advertised a web site for the make-believe company. The ad ended with the headline "What if all companies sold products like tobacco." The ad generated extraordinary traffic to the web site and became an industry sensation as advertising critics lauded its breakthrough approach.

As with all true breakaway brand campaigns, the most important fact about the truth campaigns is that *they work*. Over the past six years, since truth's launch, youth smoking in America has declined significantly. Exhaustive research by American Legacy Foundation scientists has proven that 25 percent of these smoking-rate declines can be directly attributed to the truth branding campaign. Over 300,000 lives have been saved and billions of dollars of health care costs avoided. The facts are clear: The more teens see the "truth," the less likely they are to smoke.

UNDER THE HOOD OF A BREAKAWAY CAMPAIGN

In Chapter 3, we talked about the way in which Volkswagen drove a wedge between the Japanese and German automakers to create a category of one—a German-engineered car that was fun to drive yet affordably priced. Under the slogan "Drivers wanted," VW launched a breakaway campaign in 1995. After ten years, it continues to run. The slogan is the most recognized in the automotive industry, and the campaign is one of the most admired in advertising.

From the very beginning, the master plan of the campaign was to revitalize VW sales and build a rejuvenated brand image.

When we first started working with Volkswagen, agency personnel lived and breathed the product, driving Volkswagens for over 50,000 miles around the U.S., visiting 95 of the top 100 VW dealers, and talking with over 500 dealers in total.

That provided one perspective, but the other side of the story was just as important—the consumers and their perceptions of the product. Extensive research led to consumer insight suggesting that the Japanese driving experience, while nice, mainly appealed to "passengers"—but the German driving experience attracted "drivers."

What exactly did "drivers" mean?

Research showed that Volkswagen drivers could be differentiated from average drivers. They are five to ten years younger than typical drivers, more of them went to college, and more of them have a higher household income. Volkswagen drivers also have a different mindset from typical drivers. They enjoy taking risks, they exercise more—and they love to drive. They enjoy challenging roads. They don't view cars as just a way to get them from place to place. They don't always obey speed limits. And they never, ever want to be seen as conformists.

Volkswagen drivers, it appears, are young at heart regardless of their chronological age. They are affluent without the attitude, and they are spirited nonconformists. When it comes to driving, they appreciate German engineering and are willing to pay a little more to enjoy it. That led to a mantra for this driver: "On the road of life there are passengers and there are drivers."

The winning brand positioning: Volkswagens were more drivable and individual than the boring Japanese or cheaper American models, yet more affordable and likeable than the overpriced European models. The bottom line: Your VW was a member of the family who lived in the garage.

Volkswagen's Brand Truth

Rational	Emotional
The only brand offering the benefits and "feeling" of German engineering within reach	Excitement
More feeling	Different driving feeling
More connected	Different way of living
More fun	
More alive	

"Drivers wanted."

From the brand positioning, the Volkswagen brand truth emerged. On the rational side, Volkswagen is the only brand offering the benefits and "feeling" of German engineering within reach. On the emotional side, the Volkswagen brand represents excitement, a different driving feeling, and a different way of living. Driving a Volkswagen is fun, and makes you feel more connected and more alive.

These words are the platform for the Volkswagen brand and its unique style of advertising and promotion. Forming an emotional connection with the right kind of driver continues to be the driving force behind the larger branding campaign and every product campaign that has followed over the past ten years since the "Drivers wanted" campaign debuted.

"Drivers wanted" is the anchor for the brand—not weighing it down, but keeping it focused and grounded.

Could Volkswagen's Passat model compete in a higher-priced segment? Yes, because "Drivers wanted" could speak to the same mindset in a different stage of life. Older VW drivers were about having kids, not becoming their parents.

Could Volkswagen sell the Golf and Jetta models that everyone loved for so many years at higher price points? Yes, because "Drivers wanted" could support the fact that the cars were catching up to the drivers. For these drivers, it was about getting their money's worth, not being taken for a ride.

Could Volkswagen reintroduce the Beetle, a car that would mean many different things to many different people? Yes, because "Drivers wanted" could be a platform for the car with the most unique shape in the automotive world—timeless design combined with innovative German technology. The New Beetle represented joy, possibilities, individuality—life at its best. And, as shown in Figure 5-2, its shape alone was a wonder to behold.

Could Volkswagen become a lifestyle choice? Yes, because "Drivers wanted" could apply to the experience of living for fun, not just driving for status. That meant Volkswagen could

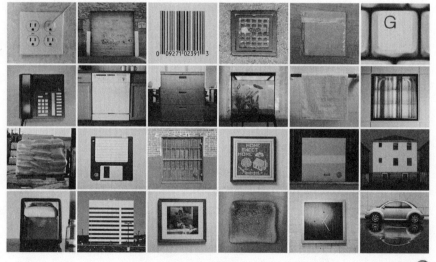

Figure 5-2 This 2002 print ad for Volkswagen's New Beetle dramatized its singular shape by comparing it to "squares." (© Malcolm Venville)

associate with other lifestyle brands—the Jetta and Golf partnered with Trek bikes and K2 skis, and the New Beetle partnered with Apple's iPod. When the Beetle needed some freshening of its own, Volkswagen introduced two limited edition colors, Vapor and Reflex, leveraging its audience's affinity for the Internet by selling these models exclusively on the Web.

"Drivers wanted" continues to be effective, regardless of the product introduced by Volkswagen. When Volkswagen brought the Touareg SUV to market, the messaging maintained the underlying brand position of a German-engineered SUV offering unsurpassed driving capabilities with superior design and technology, at a good value. Emotionally, the Touareg is a true VW—honest, more fun, and unpretentious.

The "Drivers wanted" campaign drives a brand identity that permeates all Volkswagen advertising and promotional efforts. From television and print ads, to brochures and billboards, to direct mail and online advertising, to dealer support and special events, there is a persona that emanates from the "Drivers wanted" tag line that always appears with the VW logo—a look and feel that is distinctly, recognizably, consistently Volkswagen. It is one of the best examples of a breakaway campaign introduced in the past decade.

SUSTAINED SUCCESS THROUGH BREAKAWAY CAMPAIGNS

We hope the campaigns we've shared in this chapter prove that breakaway brands are not fleeting. Behind these campaigns are five- to ten-year ideas that are sustainable despite market and competitive conditions. These campaigns are memorable and timeless because they are breakaway right down to their core. Every breakaway campaign is fully integrated, with the winning mindset and the product's brand truth forming a filter for every activity—print, television, online advertising, e-mail, direct mail, radio, advertainment, and nontraditional promotions. And that's why every campaign has achieved long-term breakaway success.

Chapter 5 Break Points

- THINK ABOUT IT: Which brand slogans and campaigns have stayed with you over time? How many of those slogans and campaigns have lasted more than three years? Have the campaigns, and the brands themselves, kept up with the times?

- Breakaway products become breakaway brands because of breakaway campaigns.

- The real magic is picking the core campaign that really works—the breakaway concept that becomes the driving force behind a breakaway campaign that improves year after year.

- A breakaway campaign uses a combination of coordinated, integrated media to capture the personality of the product, generate awareness among the right target audiences, and create demand.

- The breakaway campaign has the potential to catapult a brand into the culture, create an aspirational connection, and endure for many years.

- Breakaway campaigns usually target a mindset, not a demographic, and that mindset helps coordinate all elements of the brand's marketing program.

- Breakaway campaigns start out good, but they become legendary when they actually improve year after year. This requires aggressiveness, product innovation, continuous investment, and creativity.

- Most important, breakaway campaigns *work*—they deliver superior results. Isn't it surprising that more marketers don't insist on developing breakaway campaigns?

CHAPTER 6

Breakaway Packaging

Packaging is perhaps the most under-appreciated and underutilized element in breakaway branding—but it is the one factor that brand marketers can most control. The physical representation of a product or service has such importance that a whole science of corporate identity and packaging exists. In fact, product and package design is a separate business discipline that increasingly plays a decisive role in consumer acceptance of brands.

As much as 75 percent of a purchase decision is made in a store.[1] In a world where the consumer drives marketing, the role of the exterior package in the purchase decision, particularly in the retail environment, becomes crucial. While business executives may pay a great deal of attention to their brand advertising, they don't always consider the impact packaging alone can have on brand marketing and sales. The way a product is presented—both in the design of the product itself and in its packaging—can provide marketers with a breakaway advantage. Because of its influence on potential buyers at point of sale, outstanding packaging can even make a meager advertising budget go a lot further.

There is plenty of me-too, look-alike packaging that makes it difficult for consumers to differentiate one brand from another. The children's cereal aisle is littered with boxes that, while they scream out for attention, start to look remarkably alike when viewed side by side. To distinguish their brands, makers of children's cereal are trying everything from creating boxes with recognizable television characters on the outside to mentions of prizes inside. Some have even produced boxes that house and display free CDs on the outside.

The alter ego of brand packaging is the generic brand. Value-oriented consumers know that a generic brand, often associated with a particular store, can provide the same basic product as a name brand, but at a lower price. Generic brands tend to be underwhelming in terms of their packaging creativity, but that doesn't stop consumers from buying them. This "backlash packaging" presents a growing challenge to brand marketers whose flashy product package may not convince consumers that the quality of what's inside is any better than a generic brand.

Pharmaceutical companies are especially vulnerable to the generic packaging phenomenon. A consumer who is tired of paying high prices for brand-name aspirin, acetaminophen, or ibuprofen might readily accept the blandly branded generic. It's hard not to when there's a price comparison sign on the shelf staring the consumer in the face.

Nevertheless, for brand packaging to be effective, it needs to call out to the appropriately targeted consumer. In fact, it must figuratively jump off the shelves, as Paco Underhill says in his landmark book, *Why We Buy*: "Store displays can be remade to allow shoppers to touch and try the merchandise. But if product packaging doesn't change as well, a great many opportunities will continue to be lost. In the health and beauty aisles, for instance, smell and touch are vitally important."[2]

Breakaway Packaging Can Make or Break a Product

Packaging is everything in impulse buying categories. In grocery stores, for example, more than half of all purchases are unplanned, according to industry studies. Given that a typical grocery store stocks some 50,000 items, breakaway packaging could ultimately determine a product's success.

According to *The Wall Street Journal*, the issue is even more challenging in today's superstores, where consumers can choose from up to 100,000 different items. Spending on in-store promotions is an increasing part of a brand-marketing budget. What are major marketers doing about it? Deborah Ball writes: "When Procter & Gamble launched a new version of Tide laundry detergent containing Downy fabric softener this fall, it made deals with Wal-Mart, Kroger and others to set up in-store displays with pillows, posters and balloons."[3]

Packaging is everything in impulse buying categories. In grocery stores, more than half of all purchases are unplanned.

Consumer packaged goods companies such as Procter & Gamble (P&G) know what breakaway packaging and in-store promotion can mean to a product's success. P&G, one of America's brand powerhouses, markets hundreds of brands in 140 countries. P&G's research into consumer brands and product packaging is unparalleled.

P&G innovates in product packaging, and also in how products are displayed. In its Cincinnati headquarters, P&G conceptualizes what grocery and drugstore shelves should look like. In the ideal scenario, P&G would be able to control the look and layout of shelving and the accompanying signage so its products would achieve most favored positioning.

P&G launched Pringles in 1968 as the only potato chip packaged in a can, deviating from every other potato chip brand, each of which was packaged in bags. "Pringles Prints" is another packaging innovation—it marks the first time words and images have been printed on potato chips. According to P&G, 275 million Pringles are consumed every day. Pringles isn't merely a snack food—it is one of P&G's stable of billion-dollar brands.

Breakaway packaging offers a direct emotional connection between the product and the target consumer. It creates a sensory experience that may involve touch, sight, sound, smell, and taste. Ron Lawner, Chairman and Chief Creative Officer of Arnold Worldwide, thinks packaging can make or break a brand. "I always thought Polaroid had one of the best ideas—instant photography," says Lawner, "but they killed it by putting it in big, ugly packaging. By the time they figured it out, it was too late.

Examples of Breakaway Packaging

- **Altoids**   Mints in a tin

- **Coke**   The world famous bottle

- **Dunkin' Donuts**   Munchkins donut holes

- **Freixenet**   Black sparkling-wine bottle

- **Hanes**   "L'eggs" hosiery

- **Heineken**   Keg can

- **Life Savers**   Candy with a hole

- **McDonald's**   Happy Meals

- **Pringles**   Potato chips in a can

- **Smartfoods**   Black popcorn bag

- **Silk**   Refrigerated soy milk carton

- **Talbots**   The red door

- **Tiffany**   "Tiffany blue" box

"Apple, on the other hand, designs every product as if it is a work of art. Their computers, the iPod, all great packaging design," says Lawner. "I'd buy any product—a phone, a stereo, anything—from Apple because I know it will be well designed." Breakaway packaging often involves firsts. Some of them can be risky. Black has long been a cautionary color in food packaging because of its various negative associations—among them, dirt and death. This didn't stop Smartfoods from packaging its popcorn in black bags—differentiating itself at the time from all other snack foods and launching a new breakaway brand. Now owned by Frito-Lay, the Smartfoods brand is still distinguishable by its black bag. In the beverage industry, Freixenet had similar success packaging its sparkling wine in black bottles.

Heineken wanted to change the perception that a quality imported beer had to come in glass bottles. It was a risky gambit, because cans were considered below the status of a premium beer. Heineken broke the mold in 1999 by introducing the "keg can," an aluminum can that resembled the larger keg that carried Heineken to market. The keg can was unique to Heineken and was readily accepted by beer drinkers.

In 1969 Hanes wanted to market its hosiery to the masses. The best way to penetrate the low-end retail market was to break through with packaging that would set Hanes apart from its competitors on store shelves. The company inserted its hosiery into egg-shaped packaging and named it "L'eggs." The product was so successful that in 1972, Hanes spun off the brand as a separate division, L'eggs Products.

In 1972 Dunkin' Donuts packaged a successful product out of waste. The company took the discarded part of the donut, the hole, and sold it as a " Munchkin." Munchkins receive an extra marketing push during select holidays. At Halloween, for instance, Munchkins are packaged in special seasonal "Trick or Treat" boxes. According to Dunkin' Donuts, over

22 million Munchkins—450,000 boxes—are sold during a typical Halloween.

Sometimes a consumer's shopping experience can be defined by packaging. Soon after Tiffany & Company was founded in 1837, a distinctive shade of blue became the firm's trademark color. Representative of Tiffany's reputation for quality and craftsmanship, "Tiffany Blue" is still used today on boxes, shopping bags, catalogues, and brochures, distinguishing the retailer from its competitors. The Tiffany Blue Box became legendary when, in 1906, *The New York Sun* said in an article: "The rule of the establishment is ironclad, never to allow a box bearing the name of the firm, to be taken out of the building except with an article which has been sold by them and for which they are responsible."[4]

The Product *Is* the Packaging

We told the stories of how JetBlue launched a breakaway airline in Chapter 3, and how Silk soy milk entered the market with a breakaway product in Chapter 4. Integral to the success of these launches was breakaway packaging.

The airline industry is generally pretty tame, but some carriers have been breakaway packagers. An early innovator was now-defunct Braniff. Apparently, Braniff's management fell in love with Alexander Calder's modern-art style in 1972 and bought 50 paintings for its corporate offices. Calder's vivid artwork was then applied to the airplanes themselves. A few other airlines have since copied the idea and painted their airplanes with colorful imagery.

JetBlue, however, has managed to package not just its planes, but its entire product offering. The exterior of every plane has a blue tail. The interior of every plane has the same uniform appearance, from the elegant leather seats to the televisions in every seat back, equipped with DIRECTV satellite service—a first in the industry. The airline named its frequent traveler program "trueBlue." The online store ("shopBlue") stocks a full line of JetBlue merchandise, all of it on-brand. JetBlue has the look and feel of a very well coordinated total package.

For White Wave, the creator of Silk soy milk, packaging was a launching pad for the product. Previously, all soy milk was packaged in rectangular boxes to fit on grocery shelves. Only Silk soy milk is packaged in milk-style cartons to compete with traditional milk in the refrigerated dairy case. Silk gets maximum mileage from its packaging, using it as table-top "billboards" and as the primary image on outdoor billboards (as shown in Figure 6-1). Each carton carries bright full-color photography—unusual for milk cartons—in addition to esoteric, engaging facts about everything from Ben Franklin to wind power. This assures that a Silk carton sits on the breakfast table as long as possible.

WHAT CAN BROWN DO FOR YOU?

Service companies can also leverage breakaway packaging. UPS, the world's largest package delivery company, used an element of its corporate packaging that already existed to distinguish itself from its competition. The ubiquitous brown truck and delivery person clad in a brown uniform led the company to launch a major advertising campaign themed, "What can BROWN do for you?" John Beystehner, Senior Vice President of Sales and Marketing for UPS, discussed the strategy in 2003.

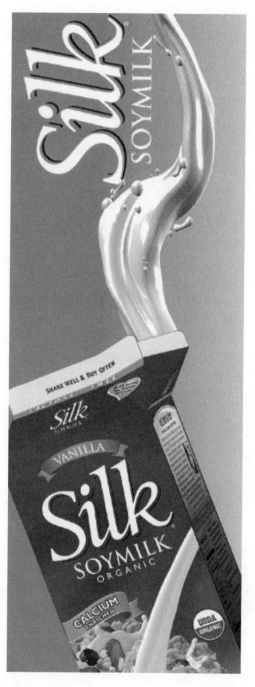

Figure 6-1   Silk's packaging is featured prominently in billboard advertising.

Our challenge was to find a simple communications message, but still make it powerful for each of the customer segments. The answer became… "Brown." It's a color unique to UPS, and ubiquitous with the UPS brand.

For UPS…and probably for only UPS…brown brings clarity as a symbol of the company's long-held, favorable attributes—reliable, trustworthy, practically wise, friendly and approachable. We discovered brown delivered for UPS a power of the familiar and personal that couldn't be underestimated—much the same as Coca-Cola red or IBM blue.

But most encouragingly, we found that brown could be used to connect the positive UPS attributes with the new story we had to tell. And it could associate new attributes with our brand like agile, innovative, business savvy, and worldly. And brown would be a vehicle that would let us engage new and existing audiences with highly relevant messages, and do so within a single, unified campaign.

So, that's how the Brown advertising campaign, which was launched last spring, came about.[5]

What better way to demonstrate that "the product is the packaging" than to look at two products whose packaging turned them into breakaway brands?

ALTOIDS

In the 1800s, the London confectionery firm Smith & Company created a lozenge intended to relieve intestinal discomfort. Named "Altoids," the product was originally packaged in cardboard cartons. In the 1920s, Altoids advertising began to use the phrase "Curiously Strong" and, more important, the packaging changed from cardboard to metal tins.

This move was a pivotal point in the life of the product. Altoids' packaging became a differentiator so unique that the company says people have saved the tins and used them for everything from the storage of nails and coins to emergency wilderness stoves.

Altoids has capitalized on the packaging by creating a line of products, each in its own distinctive tin. The tins are a throwback to the '20s, with old-fashioned lettering and embossed metal designs. Altoids Mints appear in a rectangular tin, while Altoids Sours are packaged in round tins. Altoids Chewing Gum extends the line with a smaller oblong tin. Altoids Strips, packaged in a small tin package designed to dispense the strips one at a time, won an award as one of the best packages of the year in 2003 from the Institute of Packaging Professionals. Altoids has even produced special edition tins to appeal to the collectibles market.

The product tins have been the focal point of on-street promotions and advertising. During its original launch campaign for Peppermint Altoids, a modest advertising budget was used creatively to break through in select markets. The advertising had a vintage flavor in keeping with the old-time look of the tin itself. One print ad showed only the tin with the headline, "Mints So Strong They Come in a Metal Box." The product was promoted by ad agency Leo Burnett in quirky ways: A tugboat in New York harbor was painted with the Altoids slogan, "Curiously Strong." A Chicago train was adorned with the headline: "Mints for People Who Ride in a Metal Box." As a result of the launch campaign, Altoids became the number one mint in America.

Altoids' packaging became a differentiator....
The product tins have been the focal point of
on-street promotions and advertising.

ABSOLUT

ABSOLUT Vodka entered the U.S. market in 1979. The makers of this Swedish beverage had to convince prospective drinkers that it stood apart from other vodkas. The company decided to take a risk by marketing not the product inside the bottle, but the bottle itself. The first ad, created by ad agency TBWA\Chiat\Day, ran in 1980 with a picture of the bottle and the headline "ABSOLUT PERFECTION." From then on, the bottle—and subsequently the shape of the bottle—has become the centerpiece of uniquely provocative and visually stunning print ads. Every ad headline, like those in Figures 6-2 and 6-3, begins with the word ABSOLUT.

According to the web site, www.absolutads.com, which archives hundreds of the ads, more than 1,400 individual ads have been produced since 1980 in a campaign that still runs today. The creativity applied to the campaign has involved outstanding photography, commissioned illustrations, limited edition series, and special production techniques—all built around the product's packaging. ABSOLUT's advertising campaign has won over 350 awards worldwide, and *Advertising Age* has called it one of the ten best advertising campaigns of the past century.[6]

More than 1,400 individual ABSOLUT ads have been produced since 1980 in a campaign that still runs today.

In Richard Lewis' aptly titled *ABSOLUT BOOK*, the TBWA\Chiat\Day executive says the campaign increased ABSOLUT sales about 15,000 percent over 15 years.[7]

According to ABSOLUT, worldwide sales grew from 10,000 nine-liter cases in 1979 to 8.5 million nine-liter cases by 2004. ABSOLUT Vodka is the third-largest premium spirit in the

Figure 6-2 One of a series that highlights cities, this 1987 ad depicts the ABSOLUT bottle as a swimming pool shape.

Figure 6-3 ABSOLUT advertising acknowledges cultural trends, as in this 2002 ad featuring an ABSOLUT bottle on its head, yoga style.

ABSOLUT ads used under permission by V&S Vin & Sprit AB (publ). ABSOLUT COUNTRY OF SWEDEN VODKA & LOGO, ABSOLUT, ABSOLUT BOTTLE DESIGN AND ABSOLUT CALLIGRAPHY ARE TRADEMARKS OWNED BY V&S VIN & SPRIT AB (publ). © 2005 V&S VIN & SPRIT AB (publ) world and the number-2 brand of premium vodka, according to Impact International.

PACKAGING FOR THE SAKE OF PACKAGING DOESN'T ALWAYS WORK

Not all breakaway packaging succeeds. If it is ill conceived, packaging can just as easily kill a brand as launch one. A good example is Crystal Pepsi. Doesn't sound familiar? Maybe that's because this product wasn't around long enough to remember. Pepsi created this clear version of a cola in the early 1990s. There was little reason why consumers would want a clear cola and the product was short-lived. It was a packaging gimmick gone wrong.

At about the same time, Coors introduced a clear alcoholic beverage called Zima. (Clear seemed to be the thing in the '90s.) While it was a breakaway beverage that had some early appeal with young nonconformist drinkers, sales of the original product diminished. Zima has been virtually invisible since the late 1990s. Only recently was the beverage reintroduced as "Zima XXX," which comes in three colors and flavors.

And finally, here's an example of breakaway packaging gone bad in an entire product category. It has its origin in questionable brand extension: fragrances inspired by motor vehicles. Harley Davidson is a motorcycle company. Jaguar is a luxury car. They both have introduced fragrances that leverage their brand names. To what end? The thought is that consumers who have an affinity with these vehicles might have an affinity for fragrances with the vehicles' brand name. We don't think so.

In 2004 "Hummer Fragrance for Men" was born. This cologne is all about packaging—it comes in a glass bottle that looks squat and square, much like the Hummer vehicle shape, with a spray cap that looks oddly like the Hummer's front grille-work. The cologne is packaged in a box using Hummer's most recognized color, bright yellow. Cleverly packaged, yes. But does the world really need a Hummer fragrance?

Creating the Total Package

There is a risk of oversimplifying the term "packaging." We have been discussing it primarily in the context of the physical manner in which a brand is presented, yet a breakaway brand is more than its exterior—it is a total package.

A total package is not merely the outside wrapper. It begins with the brand's mark—a distinctive graphic symbol, or logo, that stands for the brand. Around this symbol is built a brand identity that characterizes the brand, and supports its personality and brand promise. The packaging itself is part of the brand's identity. The physical appearance of the product, and whatever houses it, become key components of a marketing strategy.

The total package addresses the same questions as any successful advertising and promotion:

- Who is the target market?

- What truth and brand personality is the packaging trying to convey?

- What are the unique brand attributes the packaging needs to convey?

The underlying rationale for the packaging is often the difference between just another brand and a breakaway brand.

Altoids created a tin package that uniquely differentiated the product because it was emotionally right for the product. The product's personality was quirky and old-fashioned—yet modern at the same time. Somehow, the "curiously strong" flavor, combined with the mint's unique outer packaging, was a total package that made Altoids work in the marketplace. The mint itself looked like a bulky aspirin tablet—certainly not inspiring—so it was the taste and the tin that created a premium priced mint. Altoids became a breakaway brand.

The underlying rationale for the packaging is often the difference between just another brand and a breakaway brand.

ABSOLUT turned its bottle into a chic, cool *objet d'art*—a symbol of a brand of vodka different from all the rest. By building the brand image and an entire marketing strategy around the bottle and its shape, ABSOLUT hit an emotional nerve with its target audience that transcended the packaging itself—and became a breakaway brand.

TARGET: RETAIL'S TOTAL PACKAGE

More and more retailers are learning how to create a total package with their stores. Some are achieving breakaway results. Target is an excellent example.

Target grew out of a retailer that began in 1903 as the Dayton Dry Goods Company. Dayton introduced "Target Stores" as an entry into discount merchandising in 1962. By 1979 Target Stores were the corporation's top revenue producer. In 1984 Dayton merged with Hudson, another retailer, to become Dayton Hudson, the largest independent department store in

the U.S. In a case of the store concept driving the corporation, Dayton Hudson changed its name to Target Corporation
in 2000. In the past ten years, Target has approximately doubled
its number of stores, roughly tripled its revenues, and more than
quadrupled its pretax segment profit.[8] This is at a time when
the retail industry in the U.S. has been flat at best and other
discount chains have gone bankrupt.

One of the clear reasons for Target's success is that it operates
and acts like a breakaway brand. Each Target store is itself a total
package, from the bright red bull's-eye logo that appears consistently on the exterior and interior, to the way merchandise
is labeled and displayed, right down to the aisle signage and red
shopping carts. But Target goes beyond cosmetic appearances
and gets deeply into product merchandising to separate itself
from its competitors. With the brand promise "Expect More.
Pay Less." as its mantra, Target strives to provide "exceptionally
priced, differentiated product that no other retailer can match."[9]
For example, Target negotiates exclusive partnerships that result
in product lines unavailable anywhere else, from brand-name
designers such as Isaac Mizrahi, Liz Lange, and Amy Coe.

> *Each Target store is itself a total package, from
> the bright red bull's-eye logo that appears con-
> sistently on the exterior and interior, to the way
> merchandise is labeled and displayed, right down
> to the aisle signage and red shopping carts.*

Target drives the layout and stocking of its stores by analyzing the needs of its "guests" (Target's term for customers).
When Target learned that guests frequented their stores for specific consumables and commodities such as household clean-
ers, paper items, and prescriptions, the company increased the
visibility of everyday essentials through marketing and in-store

presentation. Target also invested in pharmacy technology and communication to improve speed and service, and to strengthen the relationship with pharmacy customers.

In April 2005, Target introduced breakthrough packaging in its pharmacies. Prescription medicines are now being packaged in a flat-sided bottle with labels that are much easier to read. This unique packaging also turns the traditional bottle upside down so it sits on the large cap. Target pharmacies also provide various color rings that snap around the cap so different family members can identify their own medications easily. This redesign is reportedly the first significant revamping of a pill bottle undertaken by a national pharmacy in forty years.

All of Target's external communications—from television commercials to print ads to newspaper FSIs (free standing inserts) to outdoor to Target.com—live and breathe the brand. Target capitalizes on innovation, as well; during its 2004 Thanksgiving sale, for example, the chain offered to call customers the Friday and Saturday after Thanksgiving. Customers could sign up for the prerecorded wakeup calls on Target's web site. This is a retailer whose approach to building a total brand package is right on target.

Breakaway Packaging Outside the Product World

Creating a total package need not apply only to product marketing. In professional sports marketing, for instance, each team is a carefully managed total package under the aegis of an umbrella marketer: the league. Professional sports teams have their own logos, marketing programs, and merchandise. Maybe that's why they're called "franchises."

Major League Baseball (MLB) has learned the lesson of breakaway packaging well. MLB heavily markets each baseball team individually—but it doesn't hesitate to leverage the competitive nature of the sport, either. The 2004 American League Championship Series (ALCS) between the New York Yankees and the Boston Red Sox presented MLB with the enviable opportunity of promoting the greatest team competition in sports. The storied rivalry has all the elements of a novelistic scenario—from the moment the Red Sox traded Babe Ruth to the Yankees, the legendary "Curse of the Bambino" was born. Nothing could beat the positioning of the Yankees brand, champions of the baseball world, against the Red Sox brand, the sport's perennial underdog. Even better, the 2004 ALCS was a repeat match of the 2003 showdown, won by the Yankees in extra innings of the final game.

MLB achieved the ultimate marketing coup when the Red Sox became the first team in history to win the Pennant after losing the first three games of the series to the Yankees. Not only did the Red Sox come back from being down 3-0, but they won the next four games in a row from the most celebrated (and expensive) team ever. It didn't hurt that the media, in promoting the series, showed characters from the Star Wars movies and positioned the Yankees brand as the "Evil Empire."

At the end of the seventh game, the victorious Red Sox were shown celebrating on national television, wearing their championship T-shirts and caps. The identical T-shirts and caps were available on MLB.com immediately following the game, and they appeared in retail outlets nationally by noon the next day. The same was true when the Red Sox won the World Series in four games. The merchandising value alone of MLB's League Championship Series and the World Series runs into millions of dollars.

If you get the feeling that politics has become more packaged than ever, you're right. The 2004 presidential campaign is strong evidence that the packaging of the product—otherwise known as the candidate—is as important as the product itself. Quite a bit of attention was paid to the stylistic attributes of George W. Bush and John Kerry during the televised presidential debates. The candidates' facial expressions and demeanors were as much a part of why viewers felt one candidate may have been "more presidential" than the other.

In August 2004, during the campaign, a brand consultant and a market research company jointly conducted a survey that asked voters how they would define each candidate in the context of advertising brands in such categories as coffee, cars, and technology.[10] Over 1,200 interviews were conducted via the Internet. Perhaps most interesting were the responses from undecided voters:

- **Coffee**   *George W. Bush*: Dunkin' Donuts; *John Kerry*: Starbucks

- **Cars**   *Bush*: Ford; *Kerry*: BMW

- **Technology**   *Bush*: IBM; *Kerry*: Apple

The fascinating aspect of the survey is the implied convergence of politician and brand. Associating a politician with a brand suggests that the politician "reminds" the consumer of a particular brand, or that a particular brand's attributes are aligned with that politician. It isn't a stretch to assume that the consumer might view the presidential candidate himself as a packaged brand.

The consumer might view the presidential candidate himself as a packaged brand.

Presidents of the past were certainly packaged. In the 1960s, Kennedy was presented to the public as a young and vibrant candidate—and he was the first to use a televised debate to his brand advantage. Nixon is known to have rued the fact that his five o'clock shadow and perspiring upper lip were more talked about than what he had to say during the debate. In the 1980s, Reagan was unflatteringly packaged by the media, who named him "the Teflon president." It loosely meant that controversies, scandals, and other negatives just seemed to slide right off of him. Nonetheless, his "handlers" packaged him in a positive light, as a president who was tough yet approachable. In the 1990s, Bill (not William) Clinton was ingeniously packaged during his first presidential campaign as a common man from a place called Hope—Hope, Arkansas, that is.

The bottom line is that breakaway packaging is as relevant, compelling, and essential for intangibles as for tangible products. While a great package will not overcome inherent product weaknesses, it will make the consumer take notice of the product in the first place. Breakaway packaging will also do much to support the brand promise. The way a product is packaged can help a product truly stand above its competition, and it can also contribute to its breakaway success.

Chapter 6 Break Points

- THINK ABOUT IT: Have you purchased any products because of packaging alone? Which brands do you think stand out because of their packaging? What role does packaging play in the way you market your product or service?

- Packaging is perhaps the most underappreciated element in breakaway branding.

- Packaging is everything in impulse buying categories.

- Breakaway packaging offers a direct emotional connection between the product and the target consumer.

- The total package addresses the same questions as any successful advertising and promotion: Who is the target market? What truth and brand personality is the packaging trying to convey? What are the unique brand attributes the packaging needs to convey?

- Breakaway packaging exists outside the product world—in sports, in music, and even in politics.

- Breakaway packaging can help launch a brand successfully.

- Interestingly, the stronger your brand becomes, the greater the opportunities to leverage your brand truth to be unique and to further break away.

CHAPTER 7

Breakaway Promotion

Marketers of everything from cars to cell phones and dog food to detergent think discount offers or product give-aways are great ideas. For them, that's the meaning of promotion.

But couponing, discounting, and giveaways aren't what breakaway promotion is all about. Cheapening the brand with a short-term price-cutting strategy could very well demean it. Marketers of brands like Nike look at promotion through their winning mindset filters and establish promotional strategies that fit naturally with their brands.

Cheapening the brand with a short-term price cutting strategy could very well demean it.

That's not to say that a breakaway brand won't ever use a purchase incentive to influence the consumer's decision to buy—promotions are tried and true in the right circumstances. But today an entirely new definition of "promotion" has emerged—a definition that replaces short-term price-cutting with long-term brand building.

The broader and more appropriate meaning of modern promotion includes such diverse nontraditional marketing tactics as advertainment (product placements in and sponsorships of television shows and movies), event marketing (creating and promoting special events in support of a brand), and buzz marketing (street teams and seemingly random product promotion). Some would argue that promotion is evolving into "experiential marketing," an approach that puts the brand face-to-face with the consumer.

There is such a rush to these new forms of promotion that one risks the faulty assumption that a breakaway promotion represents a breakaway brand. It is possible for a brand to grab attention by using a breakaway promotional tactic, but this temporary impact does not guarantee long-term breakaway brand status.

Marketers of breakaway brands recognize that despite its immediacy, promotion is just one component of an integrated marketing plan. As with any other marketing element, the promotion must be a good fit and have relevance to the brand's core positioning. Any promotion should help convey the brand promise clearly and consistently. While the promotional channel can be leveraged in guerilla fashion and may have a quick-hit objective, it should be no less representative of the brand than any other channel.

A nontraditional promotion may break through, but it may also degrade the brand image. A brand marketer desperate to gain awareness could be throwing away money on an ill-conceived or questionable promotion.

Given this context, let's take a look at some of the growth areas in breakaway promotion.

Making the Brand a Star

Advertainment, or branded entertainment, is the partnership between the advertising and entertainment industries. It also includes the world of product placements, in which advertisers make deals to get their products mentioned or even featured in television programs and films. No less a marketing giant than Procter & Gamble is aggressively pursuing product placement. In 2005, P&G's product placements in television shows increased three times over the prior year. At the same time, P&G is said to be cutting back its traditional television advertising budget in favor of product placements.[1]

Branded Entertainment Levels of Attachment

- **Sponsorship** Associating with an entertainment property

- **Placement** Visual placement of a branded product into an entertainment vehicle

- **Insertion** Brand placement and product interaction

- **Integration** Brand placement and product interaction that is elemental to plot

(Source: Jordan Berman, Showtime Networks, Inc.)

Branded entertainment is growing so rapidly that industry expert Jordan Berman, Promotions and Partnership Marketing Director at Showtime Networks, Inc., defines it as increasing levels of "attachment" of the brand message to an entertainment property.[2]

"Sponsorship" is when a brand openly associates with an entertainment property (as in the "Tostitos Fiesta Bowl"), while "placement" is the visual positioning of a branded product in a television show, movie, or other entertainment vehicle. "Insertion" involves placing the brand as well as providing interaction with the product (as in the television show "American Idol," in which Coca-Cola is prominent). At the upper end of the spectrum, "integration" calls for product placement and interaction with the brand that is actually elemental to the plot (as in the movie *The Italian Job*, in which the MINI automobile played a leading role; it was woven into the story and functioned much as an actor would).

Branded entertainment is one of the fastest growing areas of promotion. A recent survey indicates that 63 percent of U.S.

advertisers had sponsored branded entertainment initiatives in 2004, and another 11 percent said they "planned to get involved" in branded entertainment during 2005.[3] While 85 percent of the survey respondents said they participated in branded entertainment in commercial television and 31 percent named movies, other media—including magazines, video games, and the Internet—garnered double-digit response. This suggests to us that the use of branded entertainment is broad and pervasive, and it will only grow over time.

The movie-advertising marriage is healthy and growing, according to *Brandweek*:

> *Hollywood releases a steady stream of about 475 movies a year. Five years ago, those movies carried a total of 98 partners. But by the end of 2003, a slightly smaller number of movies opened with 196 clients attached, an exactly 100% increase in activity.*[4]

Movies have long been subject to commercial influence—for more years than most consumers would think. In a February 2005 *New York Times* article by Stuart Elliott, Jay Newell, assistant professor at Iowa State University, cites the earliest product placement films as a few from 1896 that were created to help promote Lever Brothers' Sunlight brand of soap. In the same article, Elliott notes that most people assume product placement in movies began in 1982, when Hershey's "Reese's Pieces" were prominently displayed as a favorite food of E.T. In fact, Elliott says, "Madison Avenue and Hollywood have been working together in earnest since the 1930s—and in some isolated instances, evidence indicates, even before then."[5]

How big are today's product promotion movie deals? Take the seven-year Coors-Miramax agreement. Coors sponsors the premieres and parties for all of Miramax's film openings. In return, Miramax has agreed that only Coors brand beers will be used in the company's movies.

The McDonald's-Disney deal is just as exclusive. Kids know all about movie promotional tie-ins—they simply have to open their "Happy Meals" at a McDonald's restaurant to find toys that mimic popular movie characters. That's because a McDonald's agreement with Disney, valid until 2006, said the fast food chain got the right of first refusal to partner with any Disney-released movie. McDonald's is reportedly evaluating opportunities with other movie studios to replace the Disney deal.

McDonald's has, in fact, become a prominent player in the promotions arena. Still a traditional advertiser, McDonald's has increasingly turned to special promotions targeting youth to get its message seen and heard. Evidence of this is notable in McDonald's sponsorship of a Justin Timberlake "I'm lovin' it" tour (named after the McDonald's theme line). The tour was so successful that McDonald's extended its reach into youth music by signing the popular Destiny's Child. Other McDonald's initiatives have included a music deal with Sony and a global partnership with Chinese basketball player Yao Ming.

Television has been a platform for brand promotion since the medium's inception. In the early years of television, "Texaco Star Theater," "Mutual of Omaha's Wild Kingdom," and "Hallmark Hall of Fame" led the way in advertainment, but the incorporation of brands into programming tends to be more integrated with the shows themselves today:

- Giant Coke glasses appear on the table in front of the judges on "American Idol." Name-brand products regularly appear and are sometimes even scripted into such popular television shows.

- During an episode of NBC's "American Dreams," one of the characters decides to enter a Campbell Soup "American Dream" Sweepstakes. Campbell Soup, one of the show's sponsors, reinforced the scripted contest by running a real one at the same time. (As an interest-ing aside, the program is set in the 1960s, so this place-ment has the added value of showing the longevity of the product—in this case, Campbell's Tomato Soup.)

- ABSOLUT created a drink called "ABSOLUT HUNK" and got HBO's "Sex and the City" series to write it into its story line. The "hunk" was a male character; during one episode, his nude image was shown on a giant billboard with an ABSOLUT bottle placed strategically over his crotch.

Some television programming is being driven by advertiser relationships; for example, ESPN Shorts, running on the cable network's SportsCenter program, are six-minute sports-related films that integrate a brand or product into the story line.

Even "Oprah" is into advertainment. During her first show of the 2004 season, Oprah Winfrey made an unprecedented, spectacular offer. She gave away new Pontiac G6 automobiles to every member of the 276-person audience. The retail value of the cars was about $7.5 million, which likely makes this the biggest television giveaway ever. The promotion won the only "U.S. Media Lion" award at the Cannes Lions International Advertising Festival in June 2005.

During her first show of the 2004 season, Oprah Winfrey gave away new Pontiac G6 automobiles to every member of the 276-person audience.

Broadway isn't immune to the brand push either. The "Snapple Theater Center" opened on Broadway in New York City in the summer of 2005. Snapple, which is the "official beverage of New York City," hosts two small theaters in a building with a large promotional electronic sign. The Snapple Theater Center joins other branded theaters on Broadway. But Snapple outdid itself when, on a hot June day in NYC, the brand tried to create the largest ice pop in the world to promote its new "Snapple on Ice" product line. Unfortunately, the 17-ton ice pop fell victim to the weather. Kiwi-strawberry-flavored gooey stuff reportedly flooded the city's Union Square area.

Video games are also a growing market for advertising, as more and more game-makers offer advertisers the opportunity to insert marketing messages. This, combined with the emerging world of marketing via cell phones, opens up a new road to effectively reach the 18- to 34-year-old market.

In the sports entertainment category, promotional tie-ins and sponsorships are considered tried and true brand-awareness generators. Almost every football College Bowl has a sponsor's name attached to it. Professional teams play at named venues: the New England Patriots at Gillette Stadium, the Philadelphia Phillies at Citizens Bank Park, and the Los Angeles Lakers at the Staples Center, for example. In 2005 the PGA held the Mercedes Championship, the Sony Open in Hawaii, the Bell Canadian Open, and the Deutsche Bank Championship, to name a few. NASCAR offers the Nextel

Magazines Blur Editorial and Ads

Paid "advertorials" in magazines blur the line between product promotion and editorial matter. Some magazines stretch the limits by running stories that embed favorable product mentions. Advertisers anxious for maximum print exposure may even create their own magazines. AT&T Wireless published *mMode,* a slick publication with advertising and editorial supporting its cellular phone products. Kraft's *food & family* looks like a legitimate magazine with features and recipes—except every recipe uses Kraft products.

Cup Series. John Hancock has been the primary sponsor of the Boston Marathon for 20 years.

At Super Bowl XXXIX held in February 2005, several major advertisers decided that on-site event marketing was as effective, if not more so, than traditional television advertising. A Campbell Soup truck distributed some 100,000 samples of its Chunky soup brand. Motorola offered cell phone games at an "NFL Experience" pavilion and employed street teams with Motorola headsets to roam about Jacksonville.

Taking the Brand to the Street

Buzz marketers are literally taking product promotion to the streets—as well as to bars, Internet chat rooms, and wherever people congregate. Sponsored concerts and celebrity appearances are commonplace. Actors infiltrate such venues to "casually" turn the conversation to a particular topic that inevitably leads to mention of a certain product.

A breakaway promotion that takes the brand to the street can help launch or reposition a brand.

PROMOTING A MINDSET

Volkswagen was scheduled to bring new cars to market in 1997, but what could it do to influence sales in 1996? With the youthful mindset of the VW audience, numerous possibilities were considered. Instead of relying on the traditional auto-industry approach of a discount or lower finance rate, the company needed a mindset promotion that wouldn't cheapen the VW brand. The result was the "Jetta Trek."

The Jetta Trek was a branded promotion that linked an existing car model to the popular Trek mountain bike. Consumers could purchase a special edition of the Jetta, which included a bike rack and a Trek mounted on top of the car. Not only did the promotion feel right for the mindset, it appealed to some 15 million mountain bikers. In fact, Trek provided a mountain bike valued at $1,000 for a few hundred dollars—because they recognized that they could never achieve the marketing exposure that the Volkswagen campaign would bring.

Trek provided a mountain bike valued at $1,000 for a few hundred dollars—because they recognized that they could never achieve the marketing exposure that the Volkswagen campaign would bring.

Volkswagen created not just a promotion, but a subbrand. The Jetta Trek had its own vehicle badge and cloth interior, as well as a prefitted bike rack on the roof that held the mountain bike upright. It was dramatic, unique, cool, and very appealing.

The Jetta Trek promotion was a win-win. The consumer could buy the Jetta and get a free Trek bike and bike rack. The promotion caught the consumer's eye, raised brand awareness, and moved thousands of Jettas in advance of new model introductions. The promotion received the enthusiastic endorsement of the car manufacturer and dealers alike because it added to the value of the car instead of discounting it. The promotion changed the attitude of the company away from rebates, which had previously been standard practice. Now there was something extra added to create a differentiated car model, not a discount to cheapen the brand. Dealers loved it because the car looked great in their showrooms, and they had something no other car manufacturer could offer, since the deal was exclusively with Volkswagen.

The promotion was wildly successful. The Jetta Trek was a sell-out at the dealers, and more important, it produced higher margins on the car model, since a $1,500 rebate was replaced by a differentiated and desirable accessory item that had a much higher perceived value than it actually cost.

With breakaway promotions, success breeds success. Based on the reception to the Jetta Trek, Volkswagen reprised the concept with another car model. The "Golf K2" was offered with a free ski rack and a set of K2 skis.

More recently, VW coupled the New Beetle with the Apple iPod in a successful promotion dubbed "Pods Unite"—another unique product pairing that leveraged the popularity of two cool cultural icons (as the ad shows in Figure 7-1). Then in 2004, Volkswagen wanted to create buzz for its new high-end automobile, Phaeton. Test-drive events and special exhibits for preferred guests of W Hotels were held in four large cities. The promotion was promoted via targeted direct mail and in the hotels. Exclusive guest-only events linked Phaeton with the prestige of an upscale hotel brand and showcased the car before it even officially arrived in the U.S. In the first three months of the campaign, 1,575 test drives were completed—double the program's goal.

Volkswagen has also been a "presenting sponsor" at the Sundance Film Festival for three years. At the 2005 festival, Volkswagen had some 35 vehicles available for transportation in and around Park City, Utah, along with a "Sundance Volkswagen Lounge." The hood of a Volkswagen Jetta was autographed by 95 stars for auction on eBay, with proceeds benefiting the Sundance Institute.

Figure 7-1 This newspaper ad leveraged two cool cultural icons—the Volkswagen New Beetle and the Apple iPod—under the theme "Pods Unite." (Photo © Brian Garland)

WARMING UP CONSUMERS

On a bitter cold January day in Boston, consumers passing by the Prudential Center on the city's main thoroughfare got a highly unexpected visual surprise. There on the street was a Royal Caribbean International party—complete with a tiki bar, lounge chairs, a WaveRunner, a DJ playing high-tempo music, and six models (four in bathing suits) who handed out piña coladas and lip balm (see Figure 7-2). And just in case passersby missed the point of the promotion, there was a 24-foot rock-climbing wall, a Jumbotron playing the latest Royal Caribbean TV commercials, and the opportunity to enter a drawing for a seven-day cruise.

Figure 7-2 This branded message was wrapped around 1,500 lip balm sticks that were distributed at a Royal Caribbean street event in Boston.

The objectives of this take-it-to-the-street experience were to generate buzz and awareness for Royal Caribbean cruises, get leads and inquiries, and, just as important, offer consumers a feeling of the Royal Caribbean cruise experience, both on-board and shoreside. The event was promoted on a local radio station, via postcards mailed and handed out in the vicinity, and through signage in the adjoining Prudential Center Mall. Public relations for the event was generated through a tip sheet sent to local and national press outlets.

The event did indeed receive local and national coverage in the way of stories and photos. It generated hundreds of thousands of promotional impressions and thousands of sweepstakes entries in one of the cruise line's top sourcing markets. Total cost: less than the cost of a half-page ad in the local newspaper.

Royal Caribbean is a breakaway brand marketer that is constantly looking to be on the edge of innovation. The company was the first to experiment with a new promotional medium in Boston's subway system. Riders on the Red Line going from Harvard Square to Central Square may have been startled when they looked through the train window into the darkness. Suddenly, a Royal Caribbean "commercial" appeared in what seemed to be live action. The effect was caused by single printed images placed in sequence on a specially lit wall of the subway tunnel. The images were synchronized to the train's speed to trick the consumer into thinking they were moving—much like those image "flip books" of old.

POWERING A NEW BRAND POSITION

As a brand name, Tyson is synonymous with chicken, but few consumers realize that the company is the world's leading producer of not just chicken, but beef and pork. This led to repositioning the brand in 2004 as a provider of protein— a critical source of energy in a consumer's diet. Arnold helped Tyson take this positioning and extend it to consumers' everyday lives with a fully integrated campaign centered around the theme, "Powered by Tyson." Television and print ads humorously depicted ordinary people doing things better than others, because they are "Powered by Tyson"; for example, a mom lifts a couch with one hand to vacuum under it.

To promote the new positioning in a cost-effective and relevant manner, we suggested that Tyson become a primary sponsor of the 2004 United States Gymnastics Team's TJ Maxx Tour of Gymnastics Champions. With over three million participating families, USA Gymnastics was a perfect fit for Tyson. Gymnastics is a wholesome sport in which athletes rely on personal power and perseverance to succeed. After the USA team's superb performance in Athens, the exhibition tour was highly visible and popular, especially with America's youth. What better place for Tyson to hand out branded "10" cards, "Protein Power" rubber bracelets, the Tyson/USA Gymnastics recipe book, and product samples?

The gymnastics tour was the kickoff for promotional activities designed to closely integrate with advertising and a rebranded web site. A key part of the campaign was national product sampling. Three branded Tyson trucks, like the one shown in Figure 7-3, drove around the country handing out tasty samples and coupons

Figure 7-3   A "Powered by Tyson" truck offers Tyson product samples and information about protein.

to assure consumer awareness of Tyson as a provider of protein—chicken, beef, and pork.

Creating the Face-to-Face Brand Experience

In each of the previous examples, the tactics differ but the strategy is the same—engage the consumer in a face-to-face brand experience that transcends traditional media. This is often referred to as "experiential marketing."

Experiential marketing is the ultimate form of breakaway promotion. It has the potential to create an emotional connection and shape consumer perception in a very special way. Katherine S. Stone, former Director of Experiential Marketing at The Coca-Cola Company, puts it this way:

> *I don't believe that experiential marketing is one specific marketing tool. It's an idea. A mindset. A focus on creating fresh connections between brands and consumers out in the world where things happen. Connections in the form of experiences that are personally relevant, memorable, interactive and emotional. Connections that lead to increased sales and brand loyalty.*[6]

An "Experiential Marketing Survey" conducted by Jack Morton Worldwide, an experiential brand communications agency, suggests that 53 percent of all consumers, and 61 percent of Generation Y consumers, think experiential marketing is extremely or very influential on brand perception. Nine out of ten consumers say participating in experiential marketing would make them more receptive to advertising.[7]

Experiential marketing is the ultimate form of breakaway promotion. It has the potential to create an emotional connection and shape consumer perception in a very special way.

Coca-Cola has been an early innovator in experiential marketing. In one marketing test, teenagers in Japan, Malaysia, and Singapore could purchase bottles of Coca-Cola with no printing on them and then put them into a "Shrink Tank," a machine that allowed the teens to create their own bottle labels. At "The World of Coca-Cola" in Atlanta, visitors are immersed in the history and lore of the soft drink. They can try 23 different beverages made by the company from around the world but not available in the U.S.

Experiencing the brand is the goal of Hershey, Pennsylvania—an entire town that surrounds visitors with Hershey's brand chocolate, day in, day out, year after year. The streets have names like "Cocoa Avenue," and visitors can stay at the Hotel Hershey or Hershey Lodge. "Hershey's Chocolate World" is the town's main attraction; "Factory Works" allows visitors to experience a real Hershey's Kisses manufacturing line.

Surrounding the consumer with the brand is the point of the Sony PlayStation Experience, which debuted at the 2003 ECTS trade show held in London, England. Some 24,000 visitors were dazzled by live performances, a basketball court featuring celebrity players, interactive game demos, and more.

Automobile manufacturers have long recognized the power of experiential marketing, and not just in showrooms and test drives. Volkswagen's "Autostadt," built alongside the company's Wolfsburg, Germany, headquarters, is a $400 million complex that features waterways, parks, marketplaces, restaurants, an events center, an auto museum, and pavilions that highlight the various Volkswagen brands. Over one million people visit Autostadt annually.

Delta Air Lines introduced its new airline, Song, by launching "pop-up stores" (storefronts designed to generate buzz that are open for a short period of time) in New York and Boston, two of their key departure cities. The New York store, in the city's SoHo district, used special events and giveaways to attract over

36,000 visitors in six weeks—40 percent more than expected. The Boston Song store, in the Prudential Center Mall, replicated the Song experience with rows of actual airplane seats and a working model of the airline's in-flight entertainment system. Employees dressed like flight attendants could book visitors' flights on the spot. According to industry sources, this store brought in 68,000 visitors in just two months of operation, with $50,000 in airline ticket sales per week. Song expected to launch pop-up stores in as many as 16 markets by the end of 2005.

JetBlue utilized a more passive but still engaging technique in promoting its service out of Boston's Logan Airport. The airline saturated one of the busiest subway stations in the city with signage, purchasing every available space so there was no competitive advertising within sight. Commuters were surrounded with JetBlue messages hanging on the walls and from the ceilings. Each sign carried a simple and direct statement about a JetBlue service benefit or a destination:

> Point A to Point B without the BS.
> Friendly People.
> Low Fares.
> Leather Seats.
> Tampa.
> Las Vegas.
> The Moon. Just Kidding.

This branded series of messages was completely consistent with the airline's friendly, approachable image, and they executed this powerful out-of-home promotion with targeted efficiency. JetBlue also convinced the *Boston Herald*, one of Boston's daily newspapers, to run front page advertising about the airline that resembled a news story.

One regional marketer's use of experiential marketing has created a breakaway brand in an unlikely category. Walk into any one of the four Boston area Jordan's Furniture stores and you instantly know this isn't just about buying furniture. At the Avon store, you'll find "M.O.M.," the "Motion Odyssey Movie" Ride. The Natick store features a fanciful walk-through reproduction of Bourbon Street and an IMAX theatre. The Reading store includes an ice cream parlor tucked inside a 40-foot-high banana split, an indoor trapeze school, and jelly bean replicas of Boston's State House and Public Gardens.

The reason for all this hoopla is to turn each furniture store into not just a shopping experience, but an entertainment destination. Embedding seemingly unrelated attractions and eateries into the furniture purchasing process may seem unusual, but it works like gangbusters. After all, if you need furniture, why not make looking for it a night out? And even if you aren't in the market for furniture when you're attending a 3D movie, you're likely to remember Jordan's and return when the need arises.

Making a Brand Come Alive, Literally

Can a face-to-face brand experience breathe new life into a brand? That's what Mattel aims to find out with its "Barbie Life In Fairytopia!" tour, a two-year branded entertainment show scheduled to begin spring 2006. This show marks the first time a live person will portray the famous Barbie doll (except for an occasional store event, at which a "live Barbie" has appeared). The Barbie doll was invented in 1959 and according to Mattel, today Barbie is the number-1 girl's brand worldwide. Despite the brand's top position, however, sales have been falling. For the year ending December 31, 2004, worldwide Barbie sales had declined 8 percent and U.S. sales plunged 15 percent.[8] Time will tell if a real live Barbie enlivens the Barbie brand.

Jordan's Barry and Eliot Tatelman (known to locals as Barry and Eliot) preside over a retail empire that sells more furniture per square foot than any other furniture retailer in the country. The brothers are featured in advertising they create themselves. The family-owned business has attracted so much positive attention that it was sold to Berkshire Hathaway in 1999 for over $200 million. As we've pointed out previously, breakaway brands don't just get noticed—they build franchises of extraordinary value.

Breaking the Brand Away with Interactive Promotion

More and more, an interactive brand experience is becoming a necessary part of a breakaway brand's marketing arsenal. BMW's pioneering work with original films suggests a bright future in this area. In 2001 BMW, with the help of its advertising agency, Fallon Worldwide, started production of what became a nine-part series of short advertising films under the general title "The Hire," starring Clive Owen as a hired driver of BMW automobiles. Many of the shorts were directed by top movie directors. The films were first introduced exclusively on the Web to reach a younger audience, and later in movie theaters. The film series was as high quality as the product itself, extending the brand experience well beyond traditional media, breaking BMW away from its competition, and creating a buzz throughout the advertising world.

We'll discuss using the Internet in detail in the next chapter, but a few breakaway interactive promotions are worthy of mention here:

- Victoria's Secret had already achieved a certain notoriety for using scantily clad models in its advertising, but in February 1999, interest in the brand skyrocketed. That's when the apparel company's online fashion show attracted some 1.5 million visitors to the Internet to watch these same models saunter down a runway. Victoria's Secret later migrated the idea to television (much to the chagrin of some women's rights groups), but it was the interactive show that first broke the brand away from all competitors.

- To promote its fall 2003 collection, fashion retailer DKNY produced an 18-minute film, "New York Stories," featuring actors wearing clothing from the line. Still frames were taken directly from the film and used in print advertising and on billboards. The film was then premiered on the Internet, in DKNY retail outlets, and at select department stores. The movie's success led to a follow-up, "Road Stories," which employed the same promotional strategy. This breakaway promotion put a new face on DKNY, positioning the retailer as a cutting-edge brand.

- Jerry Seinfeld and Superman teamed up as a comic duo in a slick, special-effects ad for American Express that appeared only on the Web. Directed by noted Hollywood director Barry Levinson, the five-minute commercial showed Seinfeld and his animated super-sidekick sitting in a diner, attending a Broadway show, and strolling the streets of New York. The story line involved a DVD player Seinfeld purchased with his American Express card. According to Nielsen//Net Ratings, the ad garnered an audience of some 2.4 million at-work and 1.7 million at-home visitors during its first seven days on the Web.

- Audi ad agency McKinney + Silver created a campaign for the Audi A3 model. "The Art of the Heist" launched on April Fool's Day 2005 and used multimedia channels to cross the line between reality and fiction. *BusinessWeek* reported that Audi's venture into "alternative reality branding" involved a staged car theft at a New York City Audi dealership, complete with fictional characters, phony magazine and television ads, and mock web sites. It was all part of an elaborate game that combined live staged events with media advertising and online play. According to *BusinessWeek*, the campaign acquired more than 125,000 followers on various web sites established by Audi in little more than a month after the "theft."[9]

- The ultimate breakaway web promotion in recent years may be the "Subservient Chicken." Launched virally (promoted via Internet pass-along rather than formally), this web site poked fun at Internet porn. The site showed an actor dressed in a chicken outfit and encouraged visitors to type in actions for the chicken to perform. The brainstorm of edgy ad agency Crispin Porter + Bogusky, "Subservient Chicken" was actually part of an ad campaign promoting a new Burger King chicken sandwich. The site reportedly generated one million hits in its first 24 hours.

The Last Word on Promotion

Brands are popping up anywhere and everywhere. In an October 2004 *Los Angeles Times* article, Robert Liodice, President and CEO of the Association of National Advertisers, says it's because "[consumers] want to be involved, engaged and, in fact, entertained. In order to breach a consumer's 'initial headset barrier' against advertising, he said, the sales pitch must be 'embedded' in something more palatable, such as a TV show, a sporting event, a video game. It must woo with charm and empathy."[10]

Liodice is not an alarmist. Television advertisers already fear the impact of digital video recorders (DVRs) such as TiVo, which allows viewers to skip over commercials. Forrester Research says nearly half of all U.S. households will have DVRs by 2009.

The threat to television advertising is just the tip of the promotional iceberg. Advertisers are on a feverish quest to find novel ways to reach the oversaturated consumer, sometimes to questionable extremes. Consider the company that is selling advertising space on men's urinals. Or the online coupon service that put removable advertising on quarters and distributed them via vending machines that make change.

This is where brand marketers need to exercise caution. As they continue to break down promotional barriers, they'll likely face consumer backlash. An inappropriate promotion—one of questionable taste, or one that draws the wrong kind of attention to a brand, could easily backfire.

The Jetta Trek promotion supported Volkswagen's image rather than denigrating it. Automobile dealers talk about the thousands of dollars "in the trunk of a car" that they can lose to discounts. The Jetta Trek promotion added value to the purchase of a car, rather than cheapening it with a price reduction incentive.

The Tyson gymnastics sponsorship offered the company an opportunity to stand for something relevant and uplifting. Associating that red oval on Tyson's food packaging with the positive attributes of America's Olympic gymnasts was a powerful differentiator. If such awareness and visibility result in another penny or two per pound of chicken, beef, or pork sold, the impact is significant.

Every marketer of a brand should be thinking about how to use breakaway promotion to achieve breakaway status. Are you getting your fair share of the market? Are you creating lasting value? Are you using promotion positively and effectively?

Every marketer of a brand should be thinking about how to use breakaway promotion to achieve breakaway status.

Yet the ultimate challenge for the brand promoter may be simply recognizing when enough is enough. A breakaway promotion based on a purchase incentive can become insidiously addictive. Take the case of airline frequent traveler miles. While at first it seemed like a great idea for the airlines to reward frequent travelers, the anticipated brand loyalty effect didn't occur. Instead, frequent travelers now accumulate miles across numerous airlines, and they make things worse by holding onto them indefinitely. This creates a liability for the airlines, who need to hold a number of restricted seats open for possible frequent traveler use.

Similarly, in years past, magazine brands dug a big hole for themselves by offering gifts to new subscribers. The theory was the magazine could afford to acquire at a loss and renew at a profit. Nevertheless, a significant percentage of new subscribers agreed to the initial term and got a free gift, but failed to renew when the term expired. The free gift offer is used less frequently today as a result.

The question, then, is how do you "remove the needle" once you get the consumer addicted to brand promotion? If the consumer expects a promotional boost with every purchase, the brand marketer must understand the economics of doing this. The downside risk of an ongoing incentive-based promotion could outweigh the upside potential. Used appropriately, however, promotion may be just the thing to separate a brand from its competitors, especially if it does not cheapen the brand and undermine its value. Marketers of breakaway brands know full well that promotion is one of the most potent forms of marketing—as long as it is exercised with caution and always put through the brand truth filter.

Chapter 7 Break Points

- THINK ABOUT IT: Have you noticed brands appearing as product placements in television shows and movies? In your opinion, how effective is branded entertainment? What kind of experiences have you had with experiential marketing?

- Cheapening the brand with a short-term pricing strategy could very well demean it.

- As with any other marketing element, the promotion must be a good fit and have relevance to the brand's core positioning.

- Advertainment, or branded entertainment, is the partnership between the advertising and entertainment industries.

- Buzz marketers take product promotion to the streets.

- Experiential marketing engages the consumer in a face-to-face brand experience that transcends traditional media.

- More and more, an interactive brand experience is becoming a necessary part of a breakaway brand's marketing arsenal.

- Used appropriately, promotion may be just the thing to separate a brand from its competitors, especially if it does not cheapen the brand and undermine its value.

- The best breakaway brands integrate every element of the marketing mix, including consumer and trade promotional activities.

CHAPTER 8

Breakaway Agent: The Internet

More than any other medium, the Internet has been an agent of change in marketing. By the end of 2004, there were nearly 300 million active Internet users worldwide, with over 170 million of them in the United States (over 60 percent of the population).[1] This is just the beginning of the curve: Broadband adoption continues to grow dramatically as cable and telecommunications providers make high-speed Internet services more available and affordable. Ubiquitous high-speed access will drive Internet usage into more homes than ever, making the Internet a mainstream communication channel.

The Internet is at the center of a group called the "influentials," according to NOP World. These individuals, the most active 10 percent of the American public, generate word-of-mouth opinions and endorsements that have a major impact on perceptions and buying decisions of others. With the Internet as their research and communications center, influentials are in a powerful position to do much to enhance or damage a brand's reputation, says NOP World, who sees the Internet as a primary tool in the rise of the "participatory marketplace"—one in which word-of-mouth drives the market, and the consumer holds the ultimate power.[2]

Lest you think the impact is solely on the consumer side, there is also evidence of a shift toward the Internet as the primary source of information in the executive suite. In a 2004 Forbes.com survey of nearly 9,000 C-level executives (about 88 percent of whom worked in the United States), 50 percent of the respondents said the Internet is the single most important source of information on business. For C-level executives working in Japan, the percentage was even higher—70 percent. Fifty-six percent of all survey respondents said they respond to online advertising.[3]

All of these data points put the Internet squarely in the cross-hairs of breakaway brand marketers. No longer a tag-along tactic, using the Internet to its fullest potential is a strategic priority. David Verklin, CEO of the media firm Carat Americas, thinks the Web is at the center of "generation 3 direct marketing." He says some of the top creative work is currently being done online, not on television. Increasingly, the consumer is becoming ever more web savvy. Verklin cites as an example the fact that 80 percent of Hyundai car buyers visit the company's web site prior to purchase.[4]

Now the Internet is a launching pad for brands, as well as an essential element in ongoing brand marketing campaigns. In fact, when appropriate, the Internet can be the primary medium used to bring a breakaway brand to market. Interestingly, new mediums such as the Internet do not diminish a successful marketer's need for a clear brand truth and a breakaway brand concept. Exactly the opposite is true. The more fragmented your marketing delivery system, the more important the need for brand clarity.

Now the Internet is a launching pad for brands, as well as an essential element in ongoing brand marketing campaigns. In fact, when appropriate, the Internet can be the primary medium used to bring a breakaway brand to market.

BMW Films and the American Express Seinfeld-Superman video ad, referenced in Chapter 7, are bold examples of how far leading brands will go with Internet-based marketing. In creating a series of branded films and introducing them online, BMW raised the online marketing bar. In executing an Internet-only video ad that was as much a mini-movie with special effects as a commercial message, American Express validated the use of online marketing as a viable alternative to television.

In prior years, the high production value of such promotions would have been reserved only for television or movies. BMW and American Express made the strategic decision to invest significant marketing dollars in the Internet because of its reach and the fact that this interactive medium is not limited by television's 30- or 60-second constraint—nor is the media cost anywhere near as high as television. On the Internet, BMW and American Express could tell brand-enhancing stories in entertainment-like fashion with no time limit.

BMW has taken its online film series, "The Hire," one step further by extending it into a branded entertainment comic book series. Six comic books featuring the film series' main character are being published, each of which highlights a futuristic BMW. The comic books retail for $2.99 each.

Another clear motivation for BMW and American Express is being part of the buzz surrounding interactive marketing. Broadly defined, "interactive marketing" offers opportunities that begin with the Internet, but reach outward to areas such as interactive television, interactive games, and the wireless world—mobile handheld devices such as cell phones, PDAs (Personal Digital Assistants), and eventually, PMDs (Portable Media Devices).

Interactive marketing offers opportunities that begin with the Internet, but reach outward to areas such as interactive television, interactive games, and the wireless world.

Even "podcasting"—the practice of targeting the iPod with programs—is a nascent marketing medium. A podcast downloadable radio program can contain marketing messages. According to a national poll, some 6 million U.S. adults said they have listened to a podcast. Nearly half of them were between the ages of 18 and 28.[5]

It is often the marketer of the breakaway brand who pushes the boundaries of interactive innovation in these emerging media. The interactive possibilities are limitless, and they become very intriguing when they involve large-scale media integration.

Now Appearing Online

It will come as no surprise that the Internet is a direct beneficiary of the media upheaval we've been discussing throughout this book. Interestingly, the Internet not only allows traditional brands to market in nontraditional ways, but it also spawns nontraditional brands of its own. Earlier, we discussed eBay as a breakaway brand in its own right. It is eBay's business model, fueled by the collective power of millions of interconnected buyers and sellers, that makes this company stand apart from all others.

Amazon.com, on the other hand, is a brand that achieved breakaway status by transferring the traditional retail store model into an Internet-only behemoth that approached $7 billion in worldwide sales by the end of 2004. Originally an online bookseller, Amazon. com has entered virtually every product category (claiming "Earth's Biggest Selection") and remains a dominant Internet-based company in online sales. Remarkably, it has grown by building a loyal customer base of tens of millions of purchasers via the Amazon. com site and affiliate sites, not through traditional marketing.

Google is an Internet-based breakaway brand whose superiority as a search engine differentiates it from a host of competitors. Increased visibility around its successful IPO in 2004 and its entry into the Internet lexicon (for example, "I'll Google that for you") have assured Google a permanent position in the Internet Brand Hall of Fame.

The Internet has created other new business models that dramatically change the way some industries operate. Travelocity, Expedia, and Orbitz are not only recognizable brand names, they represent a breakaway category: online travel agencies. Online travel has also demanded change from traditional brands: As if airlines are not under enough stress, they've had to accommodate e-tickets, online boarding passes, and airport kiosks, each of which involves a challenge in applying the corporate brand.

What have traditional brand marketers done to break away on the Internet...and become breakaway brands as a result? Following are some relevant examples.

AUTOMAKERS REV UP ONLINE MARKETING

Mitsubishi Motors, admittedly a challenger brand in the U.S. auto market, has made a strategic marketing shift, moving traditional ad dollars to the Internet. Mitsubishi had done a nice job of building overall brand awareness from 1998 to 2003, but during that same period of time, sales were flat, says Ian Beavis, Senior Vice President of Marketing, Mitsubishi Cars.[6] He suspected that people knew the brand, but not the individual car models. As a result, Mitsubishi embarked on a major effort to promote their Galant and Endeavor brands. When Mitsubishi found that almost 90 percent of their customers used the Web, Internet marketing was built into the media mix.

This led to a hugely successful campaign to introduce the 2004 Galant called "See What Happens." Mitsubishi ran a television commercial during the Super Bowl comparing the Galant in a head-to-head crash avoidance test to a Toyota Camry—but as if it were a cliff-hanger, the ad had no ending. Instead, the viewer was directed to seewhathappens.com. The web site showed the entire 30-second commercial, but with an additional 20 seconds that completed the advertising message. The site was a "persuasion engine," Beavis says, allowing visitors to discover information about the Galant for themselves. Visitors could configure and price their own cars and make a direct inquiry to a Mitsubishi retailer, thus closing the loop between promotion and the retail channel.

seewhathappens.com received as many visitors in the first 24 hours as the general Mitsubishi web site received in a month. The campaign achieved record levels of recall. The closing rate for leads obtained via seewhathappens.com was 20 percent higher than the rate via the Mitsubishi Cars web site. Beavis points out that once visitors got to the site, it didn't cost Mitsubishi anything for them to watch the 50-second online ad—and on average, site visitors viewed it 1.6 times. The initial success led Mitsubishi to create not only a follow-up installment in the "See What Happens" campaign, but a ten-city tour tied to the promotion called "Feel What Happens," during which consumers could actually try the test for themselves.

---

seewhathappens.com received as many visitors in the first 24 hours as the general Mitsubishi web site received in a month.

While the online campaign may not have turned Mitsubishi itself into a breakaway brand, there's no doubt it created a buzz that broke the car manufacturer away from the pack and galvanized interest in its products.

In June 2005, Mitsubishi turned to the Internet once again to launch its 2006 Eclipse model. The company took over the Yahoo home page for one day, using ads that allowed visitors to "drive the car around" the web page. The ads then linked to an interactive driving game.

As a breakaway brand, Volkswagen has made excellent use of the Internet. Volkswagen's award-winning web site has been a launching pad for new models and special promotions—even to the extent of selling cars online.

While the introduction of the New Beetle in 1998 had been a huge success in helping to revitalize the brand, sales had tapered off two years later and there was no "new news" about the model. In 2000, VW and its agency decided to test the viability of the Web as a buying channel and launched a campaign around two special limited-edition Beetle colors, Reflex and Vapor. Television advertising promoted the new colors and drove traffic to specially designed microsites for each color. Visitors were instructed to purchase the special editions online (they were available exclusively on the Web) and pick up their cars at a local dealer.

The unique promotion was responsible for 1,900 vehicle sales in three months. Volkswagen sold out its entire inventory of both limited-edition colors. Nearly three million visitors went to vw.com during the campaign, opening the door to future online initiatives. Volkswagen strengthened its position as an innovative leader in the automotive industry and created a significant amount of buzz within the industry and with consumers.

Volkswagen integrates e-mail and the Web into every new product launch. A minisite accompanied the introduction of the new Jetta, launched in March 2005. The site included a short film, the new Jetta television spots, and an involving interactive game, along with product information and the ability to "build your own new Jetta" online.

Other automobile manufacturers are pushing the envelope online. As mentioned in Chapter 7, Audi created a combination live event/multimedia "alternative reality branding" game with a significant online component. Even traditionally staid auto manufacturers are engaging consumers with breakaway online techniques.

Ford's Mercury division, for example, launched a series of 35 online videos called "Meet the Lucky Ones" to promote the Mercury Mariner to young females. According to *Business-Week*, the series attracted half a million viewers, two-thirds of whom clicked through to web pages about the vehicle—resulting in 500 sales.[7]

TRAVEL DESTINATIONS CREATE WEB DESTINATIONS

The visual richness of the Internet creates a powerful advertising medium for travel-related offers. Royal Caribbean International's web site, shown in Figure 8-1, demonstrates just how far the Web has come in representing the travel industry. The carefully branded site captures every bit of the excitement of a cruise, from destination videos to comprehensive itineraries. Each one of Royal Caribbean's ships is fully detailed on the site, with complete room layouts and deck floor plans. Virtual tours provide an interactive perspective on many of the ships' major features.

Royal Caribbean has fully integrated online marketing into its brand and promotional strategy. For instance, each year the cruise line runs a sweepstakes to generate interest in cruising, drive traffic to the web site, and build a consumer marketing database. The Fourth Annual "Family Cruise Sweepstakes" ran from November 2004 through February 2005. The campaign included a combination of web site promotions, online advertising banners, targeted e-mails, an e-mail newsletter, and a dedicated television commercial. Royal Caribbean also tested advertising placement on TiVo, as well as a new involvement technique called "Veepers"—customized talking e-mail postcards that participants could send to family and friends. The entire campaign was executed in both English and Spanish.

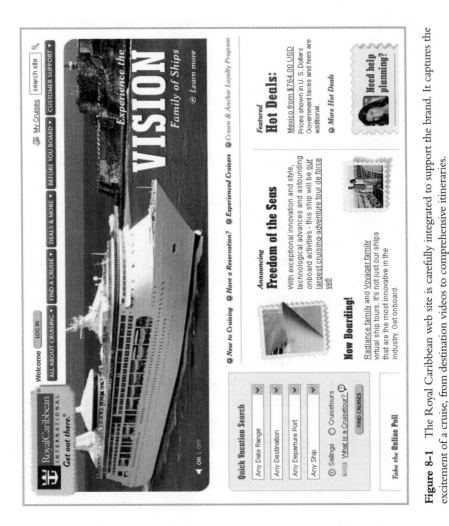

Figure 8-1 The Royal Caribbean web site is carefully integrated to support the brand. It captures the excitement of a cruise, from destination videos to comprehensive itineraries.

In another interactive innovation, a Royal Caribbean e-mail campaign promoted and linked to a rich media minisite designed to look like a cruise planner "portfolio." The minisite, shown in Figure 8-2, brought the brand to life online. It allowed prospective cruisers to click anywhere in the planner and get a real-life virtual experience of cruising—videos of the onboard experience, virtual tours of the ships, 360-degree views of the staterooms, streamed television commercials, downloadable wallpaper, and more.

Finally, here's an example of how to tightly integrate traditional direct mail with the Web. In 2005 Royal Caribbean launched a print-on-demand campaign that drives consumers to their own web pages. For instance, a prospective cruiser who requests information about a Caribbean cruise but has not yet booked receives a personalized postcard with the individual's name embedded in the copy headline. The postcard suggests the prospect visit a "personalized URL" that customizes online web content to that individual. Preliminary campaign results are very promising.

Cruise lines aren't the only travel providers making smart use of integrated marketing with a strong online component. The island of Bermuda launched print and television advertising in 2005 featuring the fact that Bermuda was "just putting distance away" from the East Coast. A visual showed a golfer hitting a ball from an office, with the ball landing on a course in Bermuda. The campaign was accompanied by a viral (promoted via Internet pass-along) online golf game that gave players the opportunity to replicate the experience.

MAK-ING AN ONLINE IMPACT IN FINANCIAL SERVICES

Prior to 2002, few people in the United States had ever heard of ING DIRECT, the operating name of ING Bank, even though it was backed by one of the largest financial services firms in

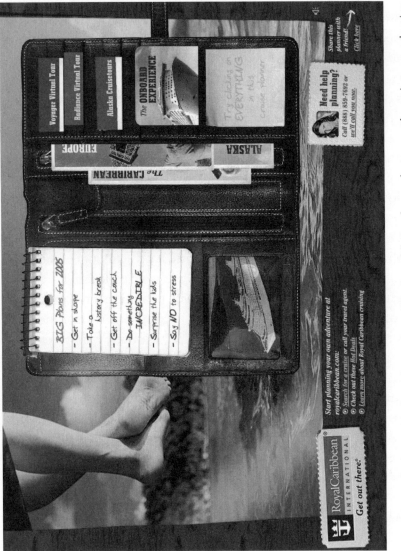

Figure 8-2 This interactive planner lets prospects "flip through" virtual pages that convey the excitement and variety of Royal Caribbean cruises. (Background photo © 2004 Michael Darter)

the world. That all changed when ING DIRECT used a combination of media, but most notably online advertising, to create breakthrough brand awareness. With orange as its corporate color and an unusual name as its lever, ING executed some exceptionally clever online work that pushed the boundaries of the Web. And now ING DIRECT has over two million customers in the United States and ten million abroad.

ING's "Orange" campaign used an online ad that read, "Start seeing ING in a new way." Not so unique in and of itself—but the ad accompanied an actual web page whose text was modified so that, for each word containing the letters "ing," those letters were highlighted in orange. While only two web sites allowed ING to modify its pages in this way, the startling effect created a brand buzz that carried far beyond those properties. According to ING's VP of brand strategy and advertising, Tom Lynch, "it scored off the charts in terms of awareness, our key brand attributes, and brand favorability, and even without a single call to action, it got very solid click-through rates."[8]

ING has continued to innovate online. One campaign offered a series of retirement planning messages positioned as purely informational, "brought to you ad-free by ING." Another campaign used a bouncing orange ball, which sometimes bounced all over a web page, to draw attention to the company's financial services offerings. The orange ball is an integral part of ING DIRECT's direct mail campaigns and it is used prominently on the company's web site. Tom Lynch says ING's online success has led the company to allocate "a double-digit percentage of its brand advertising budget to online media."[9]

ING DIRECT is a breakaway brand for reasons beyond its usage of the Internet. It is a virtual bank that does business online, over the phone, and via the mail rather than through conventional bank branches. Breaking the branch mold, the bank has opened innovative ING DIRECT Cafés in three major U.S. cities. There, a consumer can relax with a cup of coffee while surfing the Internet and learning about the bank's offerings. ING DIRECT holds seminars and special events at the cafés.

At ING DIRECT Cafés, a consumer can relax with a cup of coffee while surfing the Internet and learning about the bank's offerings.

ING DIRECT has also innovated on the product side, offering the Orange Savings Account with no fees, no minimums, and one of the best rates in the U.S., says the company. The Orange Mortgage has a simple application and no fee for applying.

BROADBAND PHONE COMPANY
FINDS CONSUMERS ONLINE

Nielsen//Net Ratings, a company that analyzes web usage, uncovered an interesting fact when they looked at online advertising growth across industries for 2004. It turned out that the telecommunications industry, although it was fourth in online advertising, was the fastest growing industry year-over-year in online advertising. That's faster than financial services, retail, automobiles, pharmaceuticals, or any other industry.

The wireless service segment was at the top of the list. But it was a company named Vonage that accounted for 10 percent of the overall online ad impressions for all phone companies in 2004, said Nielsen//Net Ratings. That was second only to telco giant SBC Communications, with 32 percent of online ad impressions.

We noted in Chapter 4 that Vonage is a breakaway product, and it has used the Internet to fuel its exceptional growth.

Founded in January 2001, Vonage quickly took the leadership position in a new technology category: broadband telephone service, or "Voice over IP" (VoIP). Given the fact that the prospective user needs to have broadband, and therefore an Internet connection, it makes a lot of sense that Internet-based advertising has proven to be efficient for the company. In effect, Vonage changed the marketing paradigm by initially using online advertising instead of conventional media to dramatically grow its business.

This is a breakaway brand that hasn't been shy about getting the message out—more than half of Vonage's 2004 advertising budget was reportedly invested in online advertising. According to TNS Media Intelligence/CMR, Vonage spent some $25 million for online advertising in the first five months of 2004 alone.

With other telcos and Internet service providers entering the VoIP market, part of the Vonage strategy was to use online advertising to outmaneuver its competitors. The medium is immediate, measurable, and targets the right kind of consumer. According to *BtoB* magazine, a portion of Vonage's online spending was in behavioral targeting—serving up ads to consumers based on their real-time online behavior.[10]

For Vonage, the Internet acts as both a brand awareness medium and lead generation engine—putting the company squarely in the forefront of breakaway interactive marketing.

PHARMACEUTICALS DISCOVER INTERACTIVE MARKETING

There has been a veritable explosion in Direct to Consumer (DTC) pharmaceutical advertising. In fact, the pharmaceutical industry as a whole is moving aggressively toward marketing major branded products on a global basis, according to IMS Health, a leading supplier of market research to the global pharmaceutical industry. One reason for this dramatic growth is the need to achieve maximum success with a branded drug before its generic version becomes available.

Pharmaceutical manufacturer AstraZeneca began marketing Prilosec, an anti-reflux drug, as the "purple pill." When the company introduced Nexium, Prilosec's replacement, it continued to market the drug as the "purple pill," using purplepill .com to do so. The web site became the fulfillment vehicle for a major promotion offering a seven-day free trial coupon. AstraZeneca recognized the value of creating a brand association with "purple pill," which was transferable from one brand name to another.

Increasingly, pharmaceutical companies use web sites, online advertising, and e-mailings because they need to convey a lot of information quickly and cost-effectively. The Web is a weapon employed to break drug brands away from their competition by both informing medical professionals and influencing consumers. Some DTC pharmaceutical web sites, such as Claritin .com, provide such extensive information that they resemble medical authorities on a particular malady. Claritin.com provides an allergy profiler and offers consumers the ability to sign up for a weekly e-mail that reports the pollen count for any zip code.

Another technique is a nonbranded web site sponsored by a pharmaceutical company as a public service in an effort to educate consumers and, ultimately, promote awareness and trial of a particular drug. For example, Quit.com is sponsored by GlaxoSmithKline, manufacturer of several products designed to help smokers stop. Quit.com offers smokers such tools as a savings calculator, dependency quiz, and quit lists and pledges.

When "Viral" Is a Good Thing

Viral marketing is an intriguing part of the Internet's power to reach large numbers of people quickly and inexpensively. Quit .com offers smokers "buddy e-cards" that they can e-mail to their fellow smokers. At the bottom of the purplepill.com home page is an innocent little link, "Send This Page to a Friend." Click it and a pop-up box asks: "Do you know friends, coworkers or family members who could really use this information? We'll make sure they get it!" This is followed by a place to enter your e-mail address and the e-mail address of someone else. Click Submit, and you have just participated in viral marketing.

What does viral marketing have to do with breakaway brands? Combine the massive media shift toward word-of-mouth with the elegant simplicity of passing along information electronically and you have a tantalizingly powerful means of brand marketing. Even such marketing giants as Procter & Gamble have begun to use pass-along e-mails to spread information about mundane products like toothpaste and detergent.

Combine the massive media shift toward word-of-mouth with the elegant simplicity of passing along information electronically and you have a tantalizingly powerful means of brand marketing.

"Subservient Chicken," referenced in the last chapter, generated one million hits in its first 24 hours. This minisite, loosely connected with the launch of a Burger King chicken sandwich, was promoted only via Internet pass-along. An Internet-based parody of the song "This Land Is Your Land," in which George W. Bush and John Kerry took jabs at each other, spread virally over the Web during the 2004 presidential campaign. It was reportedly downloaded over 25 million times and was featured on national television.

Some believe Howard Dean became a breakaway political "brand" largely because his message spread virally across the Internet. Dean raised in excess of $6 million, most of it through his web site. Both Kerry and Bush used active web sites and blogs (short for weblogs, periodic informal commentary posted on the Web) to report up-to-the-minute developments. Each campaign made extensive use of e-mails, urging supporters to pass them along to others.

American Legacy Foundation's antismoking "truth" campaign, discussed in Chapter 5, consistently capitalizes on the buzz factor via integrated marketing that includes the online channel. A spoof TV commercial compared tobacco companies to a fictional company, "Shards o' Glass," selling freeze pops containing dangerous pieces of glass. The company's web site, shown in Figure 8-3, was also a hoax. It was featured in the commercial, which ran during the 2004 Super Bowl. Right after the commercial aired, the web site received an astounding 7,734 hits per second, according to American Legacy Foundation. Previously, truth web sites had averaged 15 to 20 hits per second. "Shards o' Glass" received two mentions in *TV Guide* and became one of the most talked about subjects on blogs the day after the Super Bowl.

It is this kind of incredible instant impact that a breakaway brand can achieve with cleverly integrated Internet marketing. And when you connect the Internet with other interactive media—instant messaging, cell phones, and interactive games, for example—you have an emerging powerhouse means of differentiating a brand, particularly among younger consumers.

For example, Kellogg's connected its Pop-Tarts brand with the runaway success of the "American Idol" television show in

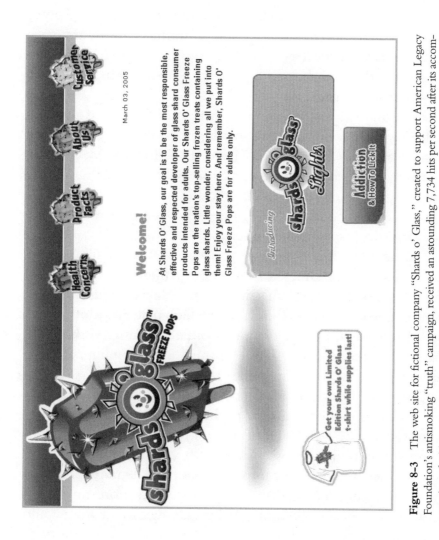

Figure 8-3 The web site for fictional company "Shards o' Glass," created to support American Legacy Foundation's antismoking "truth" campaign, received an astounding 7,734 hits per second after its accompanying television commercial ran during the 2004 Super Bowl.

a unique promotion. By sponsoring the show's 2003 and 2004 concert tours, Kellogg's obtained the right to sell tickets in advance only to consumers who knew a secret password that appeared on the Pop-Tarts web site. Buzz for the advance sale was created via product packaging and in online communities via chats and instant messaging. By getting kids to pass along their messaging, this brand stood out, even though it is in a relatively low-interest category.

In an unusual dual promotion, McDonald's teamed up with WildTangent, an online game producer, to create online demo versions of games that included McDonald's products. McDonald's gave away the games as prizes in a Monopoly game contest, while WildTangent used the same demos to sell full versions of its games at its web site. The Monopoly game itself was executed as both an in-store promotion and online version.

The next frontier in the interactive space may well be online gaming. David Verklin, CEO of Carat Americas, sees a global gaming market so huge that it will have social implications in some countries. He cites the fact that a high percentage of Korean youngsters are already addicted to online gaming. Verklin says marketers need to watch online gaming and gambling, as these could be the key to the interactive future.[11]

This could be a main reason that brand marketers are increasingly including online gaming in their media plans. One survey indicated that 24 percent of U.S. advertisers participated in branded entertainment associated with video games in 2004.[12] Gaming penetrates deeply into such desirable demographic segments as young males. Players tend to spend more time with games than they do watching TV. Leveraging this medium could bring breakaway brand status to marketers who can't afford to invest in more expensive media.

Technologies such as Mobot promise a marketing future in which consumers will interact with brands whenever and wherever they want. Mobot combines visual search technology with camera phones. For example, a consumer points her camera phone at a brand logo on a billboard, an ad in a magazine, or product packaging, and shoots. The image is transmitted to Mobot, and a text message or e-mail is sent to the consumer, offering her more information about the product. Suppose the consumer wants to place an order for a product. She points, shoots, and is directed to an online vendor who can fulfill the order instantly. It's the ultimate interactive impulse buy.

Imagine the buzz value of such technology when teenagers try it...and it works. The ability to point, shoot, and get an immediate response from a brand is so compelling a concept that it could spread virally like wildfire.

In fact, cellular phones themselves represent a new market for breakaway branding through Mobile Virtual Network Operators (MVNOs). These are mobile operators that do not own their own spectrum and, in many cases, do not have their own network infrastructures. Instead, MVNOs make agreements with existing cell phone providers to use their services. The end result of this arrangement is that a brand can rapidly enter the cell phone market and become a new breakaway provider.

Virgin Mobile, mentioned in Chapter 1, is an MVNO that uses the brand status of its parent, Virgin, to break away from other providers. Similarly, ESPN announced that it would launch its ESPN Mobile service in 2005. It will be the first national U.S. wireless phone service specifically targeted at sports fans. You can expect other strong brands to get into the branded wireless space in an effort to further differentiate themselves from competitors.

Breakaway brands are interacting with consumers in novel and dramatic ways. Nike tested breakaway wireless marketing in May 2005. The company wanted to make a splash with its upgraded "NikeiD" web site, which enables consumers to create their own custom-designed Nike shoe. Nike took that concept and translated it into an outdoor brand experience. The company employed technology that allowed passersby to design their own Nike shoe interactively via their cellular phones and a giant billboard in New York City's Times Square. Once the design had been completed on the big screen, a text message was instantly sent to the consumer's cell phone. The message provided a link to the Nike site where the consumer could then buy their custom shoe.

An Online Presence Is No Longer Optional

Rarely does a brand achieve breakaway status today without a strong Internet component to its marketing strategy. In a growing number of cases, the Internet sits at the center of a selling continuum, providing a cost-effective medium for both brand awareness and lead generation/fulfillment. It is now expected that a breakaway brand has a superb web site—but it is becoming just as essential for that brand to demonstrate *online marketing* prowess. Using such elements as e-mail, online presentations, surveys, search engine strategies, targeted online advertising, and even blogs contribute to the brand's breakaway status.

> *Rarely does a brand achieve breakaway status today without a strong Internet component to its marketing strategy.*

Perhaps most important, a breakaway brand does not pursue an Internet marketing strategy in a vacuum. The Internet can and should be another marketing channel—one of ever-growing importance, but not to the exclusion of or removed from the others. In its most effective form, the Internet is a key component of a fully integrated media plan. A breakaway brand pursues online marketing as does any other brand—but the breakaway brand uses it with such strategic impact and superb execution that it becomes indicative of the brand's persona and power in the marketplace. That's what BMW Films did, what Royal Caribbean does with its web site and interactive cruise planner, what ING does with its breakaway online marketing programs, and what truth does with its offbeat web presence. These brands are just as adept at using interactive marketing as any other media channel.

The brand that today makes exceptional use of the Internet for marketing and, more broadly, interactive marketing, will become the breakaway brand of the future. In fact, by making smart, strategic use of interactive marketing, just such a brand has the potential to displace a less savvy market leader. This is one of the Internet's strategic attributes—to be an active agent in the creation of tomorrow's breakaway brands.

Chapter 8 Break Points

- THINK ABOUT IT: Which brands do you think most successfully use Internet marketing to break away? How effectively do you use electronic media—e-mail, online advertising, gaming, wireless, and so on—to break your brand away from its competition?

- More than any other medium, the Internet has been an agent of change in marketing.

- The Internet is a launching pad for brands, as well as an essential element in ongoing brand marketing campaigns.

- When appropriate, the Internet can be the primary medium used to bring a breakaway brand to market.

- Interactive marketing offers opportunities that begin with the Internet, but reach outward to areas such as interactive television, interactive games, and the wireless world.

- The Internet has created new business models that dramatically change the way some industries operate.

- The massive shift toward word-of-mouth, combined with the elegant simplicity of passing along information electronically, provides a tantalizingly powerful means of brand marketing.

- A breakaway brand can achieve instant impact with integrated Internet marketing.

- Rarely does a brand achieve breakaway status today without a strong Internet component to its marketing strategy.

- The brand that today makes exceptional use of the Internet for marketing and, more broadly, interactive marketing, will become the breakaway brand of the future.

- A new medium brings new complexity to breakaway branding. That's why the rise of the Internet makes breakaway brand positioning and breakaway brand core-campaign clarity more important than ever before.

CHAPTER 9

Breakaway Hero: The "Chief"

Throughout this book, we've discussed the primary qualities and characteristics of brands that break away from their competitors. We've talked about what it takes to become a breakaway brand—the need to have a great product to begin with, how to create a category of one, launching a sustainable breakaway campaign, flawless execution of a fully integrated marketing program, and so on.

And despite this, out of thousands of brands, only a few become breakaway brands.

Why?

One reason is, simply, that the level of commitment it takes to build a breakaway brand is missing in most corporations. It demands a commitment to different products plus all the elements we've covered—everything from breakaway product packaging, to breakaway product promotion, to breakaway advertising campaigns. It means adopting an attitude of creativity and continuous improvement. It requires a keen understanding of where the product fits in relation to its competition and its category. It requires a short-term investment in the launch and a long-term investment in a programmatic, ongoing approach to breakaway marketing.

More and more, we find that senior management plays a crucial role in the breakaway branding process. It is not just marketing management's responsibility, but all of the "Chiefs," perhaps even the board of directors, who must embrace a breakaway brand. By their collective actions and attitudes, they help turn customers, prospects, analysts, employees, and shareholders into brand enthusiasts.

More and more, we find that senior management plays a crucial role in the breakaway branding process.

Ultimately, the breakaway brand's true hero must be the CEO, COO, or CMO who shapes the company's brand vision and demands that breakaway branding behavior takes place. An advertising agency's role is often to clearly understand this mandate and to turn that direction into brilliant, breakaway execution.

The importance of the CMO (Chief Marketing Officer) title has grown significantly of late. In a recent survey of senior executives conducted by the Association of Executive Search Consultants (AESC), the top title selected as most powerful, second only to the CEO, was the CMO. In explaining the results, AESC president Peter Felix said, "The CMO is the executive who will craft messages, integrate channels, and bring in the programs that will allow for collaborative filtering—and do it on a global stage. The CMO is the leader who can make a difference between mere sales and a total marketing campaign—and help define the bottom line success of a company."[1]

It is the Chief's vision, determination, and guts that push a brand to greatness. His or her involvement in the brand—and his or her recognition of the strategic importance of branding to the company's success—will often tip the breakaway branding scale. Without the Chief functioning as a supportive leader who champions the brand, achieving breakaway brand status is all the more difficult.

Top 25 Brand CEOs

1. Dell—Michael Dell, Kevin Rollins

2. Starbucks—Orin Smith

3. Apple Computer—Steve Jobs

4. Nike—Phil Knight

5. Amazon.com—Jeff Bezos

6. eBay—Meg Whitman

7. Southwest Airlines—Jim Parker

8. FedEx—Fred Smith

9. Virgin—Richard Branson

10. Coca-Cola—Neville Isdell

11. Target—Robert Ulrich

12. American Express—Ken Chenault

13. BMW—Helmut Panke

14. Wal-Mart—Lee Scott

15. Anheuser Busch—Patrick Stokes

16. Google—Eric Schmidt

17. Walt Disney—Michael Eisner

18. Microsoft—Steve Ballmer

19. JetBlue Airways—David Neeleman

20. UPS—Mike Eskew

21. General Electric—Jeff Immelt

22. McDonald's—Charlie Bell

23. Hewlett-Packard—Carly Fiorina

24. Marriott—Bill Marriott, Jr.

25. Procter & Gamble—A. G. Lafley

(Source: *Chief Executive*, November 2004. This list is current for 2004.)

Getting It Right

Which senior executives are getting it right? A November 2004 survey of 450 corporate and marketing executives conducted by Lippincott Mercer for *Chief Executive* magazine ranked the "Top 25 Brand CEOs" for 2004 (see sidebar). It is interesting to note that more than half of the brands on this list are cited in this book as breakaway brands. Equally interesting is that many of the best-marketed companies are not what we might think of as traditional product marketing firms. You will find a wide diversity of industries and a healthy dose of Internet-based companies on the list. In fact, only one (Procter & Gamble) is a packaged goods company.

We would submit that a major reason these brands break away from their competitors and stand out as exemplary brands regardless of category is the CEO. The CEOs on the Top 25 list, and others whose brands we have mentioned in this book, know that a brand that stands apart has the potential to drive a company's sales, improve its margins, grow its profitability, and increase its market cap. Interestingly, one of the great results of breakaway branding is the power to raise prices.

As FedEx CEO Fred Smith says in the article that accompanies the Top 25 list: "One of the things that we recognized about 10 or 12 years ago was that probably of all of the assets on our balance sheet, none was more important than the brand, even though it wasn't capitalized at all."[2]

We'll revisit that theme—the financial value of the breakaway brand—in the next chapter. But for now, let's take a closer look at the specific role the Chief plays as a breakaway brand hero.

The Chief As Brand Visionary

Often it is the role of the CEO, COO, or CMO to act as a brand visionary—a leader who recognizes the true potential of a brand and is not afraid to take that brand from good to outrageously great.

CREATING BRANDS CONSUMERS LOVE

Apple Computer has been left for dead more than once in its corporate history. When Steve Jobs founded the company with Steve Wozniak in 1976, their grandiose plan to market a "computer for the rest of us" led to the birth of the first legitimate personal computer. IBM entered the PC market in 1981 and many predicted that Apple would soon fail. Yet Apple survived the onslaught of "Big Blue" and carved out its own unique niche, depending on an audience that skewed more toward educators, students, and the graphic arts.

Apple headed in a potentially bold new direction in 1983 with Jobs' hiring of John Sculley, formerly of Pepsi-Cola. Jobs already sensed that Apple needed to move aggressively into the consumer realm. What better way to do so than to bring in a consumer goods expert to run the company? Ironically, it was Sculley who then managed to engineer Jobs' ouster from Apple in 1985.

Again, it was a dark time for Apple. The company foundered while Jobs formed two other companies, NeXT Computer and Pixar (which has become the hottest company in computer animation for movies). Proving that the more things change the more they stay the same, NeXT was purchased by Apple in 1996 and, lo and behold, Steve Jobs returned as CEO of the company he founded.

This time, he'd be very much in control. As we discussed in Chapter 2, Jobs oversaw the launch of an advertising campaign called "Think Different"—as much a marketing direction as it was his own mantra for reinventing a tarnished brand.

Along with the marketing, it was the breakaway products launched under Jobs that gave Apple a sense of revitalized purpose. The iMac became the country's best-selling computer in the fall of 1998. The PowerBook, Apple's laptop computer originally introduced in 1991, was completely overhauled and relaunched in 1997/98. Then Jobs began pushing the company toward its current consumer-oriented product line. First came the introduction of iMovie in 1999, which provided high-quality digital editing to the mass market, and then iTunes, the music-playing software launched in 2001.

Perhaps most startling was the 2001 introduction of the iPod—the digital music player that has pioneered a category and gone on to become the undisputed leading brand. After just three years in the market, sales of iPod reportedly came close to matching sales of the company's flagship Macintosh business.

To Steve Jobs, though, iPod was just a natural progression for Apple. In a February 2005 *FORTUNE* cover story, Jobs is quoted as saying: "The place where Apple has been standing for the last two decades is exactly where computer technology and the consumer electronics markets are converging. So it's not like we're having to cross the river to go somewhere else; the other side of the river is coming to us."[3] iPod was credited for Apple's surging sales for the quarter ending December 25, 2004—a record $295 million, up from $63 million the previous year. Once a has-been, Apple's stock became one of the hottest of 2004 (Apple announced a two-for-one stock split in February 2005). In January 2005, Steve Jobs kept the market pressure on by introducing a $99 iPod and a $499 Mac mini-sized computer.

Jobs sums up Apple's reemergence as a breakaway brand nicely: "Apple's core strength is to bring very high technology to mere mortals in a way that surprises and delights them and that they can figure out how to use."[4]

SEEING THE BIG PICTURE IN THE CRUISE INDUSTRY

Royal Caribbean International has become the most preferred brand in the cruise industry because of its management team's common vision. CEO Richard Fain, then President and COO Jack Williams, current President Adam Goldstein, and Master Naval Architect Harri Kulovaara collectively pioneered Voyager-class ships. This management team had a vision for a new type of product that would set Royal Caribbean apart from every other cruise line. Why not change the very image of cruising and turn it into the high-sea adventure it should and could be?

The team took the bold step of building larger ships with features that had never been put out to sea—onboard amenities such as the company's signature rock-climbing walls and ice-skating rinks. This was no small task and not without risk, given that each ship is a multi-hundred million dollar traveling resort hotel.

The strategy paid off. The ships have become symbols of innovative, breakaway thinking in an emerging segment of the travel business. As a result, Royal Caribbean International has outclassed its competitors and charted a new course for the entire cruise industry.

Dan Hanrahan, formerly Senior Vice President of Sales and Marketing of Royal Caribbean and now President of Celebrity Cruises, knew the marketing had to reflect the quality of the ships. "I was the marketing guy who was the lucky beneficiary of a superior product," says Hanrahan. "The courageous work was done by the team who built Voyager. We had the breakthrough ships. What we needed to do was deliver a message through the marketing that was consistent with the product experience onboard. From there, the Marketing and Fleet Operations teams worked together to fine-tune the onboard experience and continue to make it better and better. We got to a point where everybody understood the brand so well that it was easy to decide what to do next."[5]

"I was the marketing guy who was the lucky beneficiary of a superior product.... We had the breakthrough ships. What we needed to do was deliver a message through the marketing that was consistent with the product experience onboard."

—Dan Hanrahan

Through consumer analysis, Hanrahan and his team came to the conclusion that the true audience for cruising was vibrant, active, adventurous—not the stereotyped sedentary customer. "We had done an in-depth consumer segmentation study that showed people were looking for freedom of choice. They didn't want to be confined, they wanted to have an active, fun, energetic vacation—and we were providing that," says Hanrahan. He sought and found an agency that shared his perspective on the audience and could help him build a breakaway marketing program targeting the audience mindset. The client-agency relationship clicked, and the result was a brand campaign centered around the theme "Get Out There." The campaign not only differentiates Royal Caribbean in the marketplace, it also makes people proud to work at the company.

"Now everyone understands the brand—the marketing team and agency get it, the folks on the fleet get it, the salespeople get it, the entire organization gets it. 'Get Out There' has become part of our language. We have a cool product, we do cool marketing, and it gets everybody energized.

"We didn't go overboard to get people onboard with the brand," Hanrahan adds. "The campaign resonates with people and it works. We've had tremendous results, and we're not shy about sharing them with employees. The quality of the marketing and the results are what gets everyone on the same page."

The company knows its marketing works not just with employees, but with consumers as well. That's because travel agents tell them that customers call or walk in to ask specifically about Royal Caribbean cruises. Industry studies show Royal Caribbean places first in brand preference, and first in the cruise line customers are most likely to choose for their next cruise.

Well-orchestrated, integrated marketing plays a key role in maintaining Royal Caribbean's breakaway status. In addition to some of the most memorable award-winning television advertising (backed with a high-energy rock 'n roll song), Royal Caribbean is a master of integrated collateral event marketing, online communications, direct marketing, and onboard promotion. The company is a frequent innovator in online and alternative media, assuring that it leaves no stone unturned when it comes to reaching its target audience in a highly consistent manner. "The key to integration is maintaining your focus," says Hanrahan. "If you really understand your brand, you know how far you can push it."

Hanrahan's experience on the marketing side with Royal Caribbean brings an important perspective to his new role as President of Celebrity Cruises. He advises CEOs and presidents to "be as courageous as our leadership team was when they envisioned the Voyager class, take risks, and don't be afraid to stretch the brand." It would have been easy for Royal Caribbean to be the typical cruise marketer, according to Hanrahan. Instead, the company broke the mold. "The challenge was to change everything and take a completely different route. That's the only way to be a breakaway brand—if you're willing to take those risks and not slide back into your comfort zone."

According to Hanrahan, there are three key elements necessary for breakaway branding success. "The first is a credible product. You're not going to get there without a good product, because you're not going to fool the consumer. Then you need to position your product in a truly compelling way. Third, you've got to have a management team who's willing to take some real risks. All three of those things have to come together for you to be successful."

The Three Key Elements of Breakaway Branding Success

Royal Caribbean advises senior executives that three essential elements must come together to build a breakaway brand:

1. A credible product

2. Positioning that product in a truly compelling way

3. A management team who's willing to take some real risks

ENVISIONING A WORLD IN WHICH SMOKING IS NO LONGER

When the tobacco industry and the attorneys general in 46 states and five U.S. territories reached a "Master Settlement Agreement" in March 1999, the American Legacy Foundation was born. This not-for-profit independent public health foundation has one purpose: "building a world where young people reject tobacco and anyone can quit."

It's largely the vision of Dr. Cheryl Healton, the foundation's president and CEO, that is making this a reality. And her vision has included guiding a breakaway brand known as "truth," the highly acclaimed, national youth tobacco prevention counter-marketing campaign. truth has been credited in part with reducing youth smoking prevalence to its current 28-year low.

In many respects, Dr. Healton is the ideal visionary for the task of reducing the deadly toll of tobacco. A former smoker herself, Dr. Healton lost her own mother and several close family members to tobacco-related diseases. She led grant-funded projects for the Centers for Disease Control and Prevention (CDC) to study the effects of marketing and countermarketing on youth tobacco use, developed a series of prevention partnerships linking public health researchers with New York State tobacco-health policy makers, evaluated intervention programs for the state's largest youth tobacco prevention program, and worked at Columbia University to bring an interdisciplinary approach to tobacco control and prevention. Dr. Healton is currently writing a book on the topic of women and smoking, with common-sense strategies to increase successful quit attempts.

Under her leadership, the truth brand has targeted youth nationally with an antismoking campaign that has contributed to dramatic declines in youth smoking. truth was conceived to be a brand that was cooler than smoking. It was designed to take teens' need to rebel and point it at Big Tobacco—instead of reinforcing the need to smoke, which represented rebellion and control.

The brand truth of truth became the underlying rationale for its ongoing existence. On the rational side, truth represents honest facts and information that exposes Big Tobacco and puts teens in control. On the emotional side, truth embodies such feelings as rebellious, risky, intelligent, empowering, independent, and tolerant.

A study that appeared in the March 2005 *American Journal of Public Health* showed a decline in youth smoking prevalence among all students in grades 8, 10, and 12 from over 25 percent to 18 percent between 1999 and 2002. The study found that the truth campaign accounted for about 22 percent of this decline. At the same time, however, the tobacco industry has spent more money marketing and promoting its products each year since the 1997 Master Settlement Agreement, spending $12.5 billion in 2002 alone.

Because of the tobacco industry's enormous marketing investment, Dr. Cheryl Healton feels the truth campaign must be well funded and must continue to be a breakaway brand to be effective and to save lives.

The Chief As Brand Champion

When a senior executive adopts the role of brand champion, his or her enthusiasm becomes infectious—and the troops follow the lead.

CHAMPIONS OF A BANK BRAND THAT'S ANYTHING BUT TYPICAL

Lawrence K. (Larry) Fish has reason to be enthusiastic about his brand. As CEO of Citizens Financial Group, he has seen the Providence, Rhode Island, bank holding company grow 25-fold since joining the organization in 1992. With the 2004 acquisition of Charter One Financial, Citizens Bank has about

25,000 employees, with retail and commercial banking operations in 13 states. Citizens Bank is now the eighth largest commercial bank holding company in the United States in total deposits.

When Larry Fish arrived at Citizens in 1992, he found a bank that was virtually unknown outside its New England footprint. Unlike your typical banker, Fish recognized the power of branding. "Many chairmen in the financial services industry just look at marketing as an expense line," says Theresa McLaughlin, CMO of Citizens Bank. "We've got a CEO who really understands that the brand can provide air cover to move the whole company forward. He's been a great cheerleader for the brand."[6]

Championing the brand is a key responsibility of the CEO, says Larry Fish. "I don't believe you can have a breakaway brand without passion at the CEO level. The CEO must be actively involved in all the different brand elements. Brand is about much more than just advertising—it's about the lighting in the hallway, and having the proper signage, and how we treat people in the company."[7]

Larry Fish is a committed brand champion. "Our CEO's support of the brand is pervasive and reaches throughout the organization," McLaughlin says. "You can ask any one of our 25,000 employees what our Credo is [the Citizens Credo—Customers, Colleagues, and Community—is an extension of the brand; see page 218]. Each Citizens employee will know the Credo," she continues. "Everybody in the company is marching to the same set of values. We even have 'Credo moments,' where we catch people doing something right."

"How you treat people is part of your brand," says Larry Fish. "People live the brand through our Credo. Everyone on my executive policy committee has a Credo meeting or two somewhere in our geography every month.

"You can't have a successful brand if your people aren't living that brand. If the people that represent you to the customer, and represent you to the marketplace, don't understand the brand and don't live it and believe it, you won't be a breakaway brand.

"I think understanding and living the brand is like peeling an onion," says Fish. "You're never finished. Every day you're finding a way to reinforce that brand in a different part of the company, whether it's the meals we serve in the cafeterias, or the art that's on the walls, or the attention we pay to natural light. There are just a million ways that you are reinforcing the brand, all the time."

"Living the brand is like peeling an onion. You're never finished. Every day you're finding a way to reinforce that brand in a different part of the company."

—Larry Fish

The relationship between CEO and CMO is another key to the success of Citizens Bank as a breakaway brand.

"You can't create a breakaway brand without a committed and passionate CEO," says Larry Fish, "but you also can't do it without a great CMO. If you have one and not the other, it's not going to work.

"You need a CMO who doesn't just think of the job as advertising," says Fish, "and you need a CMO who's completely aligned with the CEO."

Theresa McLaughlin is as proactive a brand champion as Larry Fish. A Citizens Bank employee for ten years and in financial services for 19 years, McLaughlin believes there is more to brand advocacy than marketing. "First and foremost, a CMO has to understand how the company makes money," she says.

"You have to be able to sit at the table with the finance people to earn the right to demonstrate that the brand is going to help the company make a profit."

The Citizens brand is strongly differentiated under the umbrella theme, "Not your typical bank." Because of a consistent brand voice, McLaughlin says, the bank has been able to maintain a separation with competitors of probably 10 to 20 percent share of voice. "Our strategy is to be out there all the time creating a buzz about our brand," McLaughlin says, "so when people are ready to buy, we're in their considered set. Integration is important as well. Consumers need to see a message three to four times, in different media, but everything needs to have the same voice."

"Consumers need to see a message three to four times, in different media, but everything needs to have the same voice."

—Theresa McLaughlin

One of the keys to building a breakaway brand, says McLaughlin, is a trusting relationship with her ad agency. "Arnold brought to life for me the whole notion of the rational and emotional," says McLaughlin. "I think many brands try too hard on the rational side, getting their product features and benefits out there. I have learned over time that it's important for us to create a brand people *like*. They're looking for the next Citizens TV spot. They get a smile when they see it—we actually call it the 'Citizens Smile.' The fact that we're human, we're self-effacing, we're not afraid to poke fun at ourselves even though we're a bank—people see a little bit of themselves in us. That emotional side of the brand has created such lift for us that we haven't had to work as hard to say we've got the better product or the better rate. It gives us the ability to break away."

A key reason for Citizens' success in brand marketing is the bank's continuous testing. "We're very consumer-focused," McLaughlin continues. "Everything we do, we test and we research. We make sure it's not just my opinion, or the chairman's opinion, or the agency's opinion, but that the target audience is weighing in. Research is critical to making sure the brand stays on the mark."

When you sum it all up, being the nice, friendly, approachable bank sets Citizens Bank apart. But reinforcing that positioning with customers, colleagues, and community is essential. That's why the bank is committed to caring about people. "Some CEOs lead strategically, others financially," says Larry Fish. "We choose to lead our business around our people and our customers. We're in a people business. And it's people who produce the profits."

DRIVING THE WORLD'S LEADING
CONSUMER BRAND MACHINE

He was called one of America's best managers by *BusinessWeek* in 2003, CEO of one of America's most admired companies by *FORTUNE* in 2004, and "growth wizard" of one of America's brightest idea companies by *Business 2.0* in 2005.

A. G. Lafley, CEO of Procter & Gamble (P&G), is widely credited with turning around the consumer products giant when he took over in 2000. While his is certainly a story of invigorating sales, increasing profit, and generally creating change, the Lafley legacy could just as easily be the fact that he returned P&G to its former luster as the finest brand marketing machine in the world.

One simple yet significant way Lafley has done that is by exhorting employees to listen intently to the female consumers

The Citizens Credo

- **Customers**   Hug the customer. Smile. Say thank you. Return phone calls and e-mails in a timely manner. Do whatever you can every day, in every way, to provide world-class service. Consistently exceed customer expectations. Always honor our commitment to customers. Give customers a reason to say, "Wow, I love these people." In short, treat the customer the way you would love to be treated all the time.

- **Colleagues**   We want Citizens to be the best place to work in the world. The environment will be extraordinarily caring, like an extension of your own family. We will be supportive in time of personal difficulty, create opportunities for professional growth, and always make an effort to listen and act on your ideas. Every colleague will be treated with dignity and respect at all times.

- **Community**   We believe great companies have a moral core. We care deeply about our communities, and we demonstrate this commitment every day by volunteering where there is a need. We respect the law at all times, and always conduct ourselves with integrity. All of our work at Citizens must be ethical and honest. By giving back, and conducting ourselves with integrity, our customers and colleagues will be proud of Citizens.

who purchase 80 percent of the company's products and know what they want. In an article about Lafley's philosophy of looking outside the company for solutions, the P&G CEO is quoted as saying "…women don't care about our technology…they want to hear that we understand them."[8]

A lot of what Lafley has accomplished in the past five years has had to do with championing several of the great P&G brands, among them Crest, Tide, and Pampers. According to a *BusinessWeek* cover story[9] about P&G, on becoming CEO, Lafley's first statement to his managers was "focus on what you do well—selling the company's major brands...instead of trying to develop the next big thing."

The problem was that P&G had no new successful brands, save one, for over a decade, and the existing brands were languishing. One way to jump start this situation was to acquire great brands instead of developing them in-house. Under Lafley's aegis, that's just what P&G has been doing. In 2001, for example, the company purchased Clairol, and it acquired Wella in 2003. Perhaps the most stunning acquisition yet, though, was the purchase of Gillette, announced by P&G in January 2005 and valued at over $55 billion.

Various sources reported that P&G had approached Gillette prior to Lafley's tenure but had been rebuffed. It's easy to believe P&G's affable CEO was instrumental in getting the deal done. In so doing, P&G extends its already impressive brand portfolio into new territory. Gillette, a brand machine of its own, is the owner of such notable brands as the Mach3 razor, Duracell batteries, Oral-B dental products, and Braun appliances. In fact, Gillette brings five billion-dollar brands to the table, which, along with P&G's 16 billion-dollar brands, creates the world's undisputed brand king with 21 brands each worth $1 billion or more.

With Lafley's renewed emphasis on P&G's core brands, things have changed dramatically. In Q1 2004, 19 of the company's 20 largest brands saw their market shares improve, according to *FORTUNE*.[10] Under Lafley, the Crest brand alone has doubled in sales in three years, says *FORTUNE*, because of aggressive brand extensions, such as teeth-whitening systems Crest

Whitestrips and Crest Night Effects, and products like the Crest SpinBrush toothbrush. Crest is now a $2 billion brand.

Other P&G brands have been getting miracle makeovers. Pringles, the potato chip in the can, launched "Pringles Prints," the first chips with printed trivia questions on them. The venerable Tide brand has undergone numerous brand extensions of late, including Tide Cold Water and Tide with Downy. Mr. Clean has seen the introduction of Mr. Clean Magic Eraser Products and a Mr. Clean AutoDry Carwash product. This flurry of brand activity has contributed to P&G's bottom line: revenue increased 19 percent and earnings grew 25 percent in fiscal 2004.

A. G. Lafley is the brand champion behind it all. As *Business-Week* said when it proclaimed Lafley a top manager: "...Lafley believes that there's still tremendous growth in the core brands. He has made one thing clear: P&G's stodgy corporate culture is gone for good."[11]

CREATING ADVERTISING THAT CHAMPIONS BREAKAWAY BRANDS

Ron Lawner is the Chairman and Chief Creative Officer of Arnold Worldwide. He has built an impressive list of high-profile branding campaigns that have garnered virtually every prestigious industry award. But after more than 30 years in the advertising business, Ron can remember only a few times clients have let him "swing for the fences."

"Brands are wonderful things that should be cherished," says Lawner, "but there's a lack of joy in branding. It's heartbreaking how many brands don't get their due. I think of brand advertising as an art, but I haven't found a lot of art lovers in corporate America."[12]

The problem, according to Lawner, is that many corporations are driven by fear and a short-term focus on the bottom line. Not enough heads of marketing are willing to take risks to do great work, and not enough CEOs know what great work is. "Companies can be straight-jacketed by their own cultures," he says.

But Lawner also believes that when the client has a vision and the courage to go for it, an advertising agency can do great work—and that's what helps make a breakaway brand. With the "right DNA" in the agency-client partnership, magic occurs. "It's like the sperm finding the egg," he jokes. "When it works, it's a beautiful union."

From an advertising perspective, what is it that makes a breakaway brand stand out from all others? Lawner says the key is for the brand advertiser to understand and respect the consumer. "Great brands do advertising that is intelligent, honest, approachable. Great brands lead the consumer. The advertising is aspirational, and the brand becomes the consumer's friend.

> *"Great brands do advertising that is intelligent, honest, approachable. Great brands lead the consumer."*
>
> **—Ron Lawner**

"When the consumer identifies with the brand, there's an emotional connection," Lawner continues. "Just like fans root for sports teams, consumers root for brands. They'll even be forgiving if the brand screws up because they like it so much."

Lawner was the originator of the renowned Volkswagen tagline, "Drivers wanted." He has played a guiding role in the award-winning Volkswagen work for ten years. He still finds the brand fresh and contemporary. "When Volkswagen introduced the New Beetle, it was a breakaway design—something round in a square world," says Lawner. "They weren't afraid to take a risk.

The advertising is like that, too. It doesn't sell out—it still has that special brand voice. It creates an insider dialog with the consumer."

For most advertisers, it isn't easy to create breakaway advertising. "Some brands think they can buy market share by dominating the marketplace with advertising," says Lawner. "They try to buy the consumer's loyalty. But they're disingenuous, and the consumer knows it. The breakaway advertisers know they have to get the consumer to really connect with their brands. You've got to get a lot of things right. You should never stop trying to make the advertising better."

One of Ron Lawner's favorite quotes sums up his view toward what's needed to succeed in breakaway advertising:

Everything wants to be mediocre, so what it takes to make anything more than mediocre is such a f***ing act of will.

—Ira Glass,
host of "This American Life," NPR

The Chief As Breakaway Brand Architect

A Chief has the opportunity to be a primary architect of the breakaway brand—and when that happens, the possibilities are limitless.

LAUNCHING A BREAKAWAY AIRLINE

"The JetBlue brand was built on giving Customers the things they want, and nothing they don't. We also added a little style and an honest and humorous voice to our marketing so our Customers know real people are running this shop." This excerpt from the *JetBlue 2002 Annual Report* is as telling of the fledgling airline's success as it is indicative of David Neeleman's leadership as CEO of JetBlue.

It's no accident that the annual report emphasizes the word "Customers." When Neeleman launched JetBlue in early 2000, Customer service with a capital "C" was paramount amongst his goals. No other start-up airline offered customers electronic ticketing, no requirement for a Saturday night stay, new planes, or leather seats with free satellite TV on every seatback. Oh, and did we mention low fares?

David Neeleman knew that's what it would take to be a different kind of airline. He had cofounded Morris Air and sold it to Southwest. He stayed at Southwest just long enough to learn what they were doing right to revolutionize the airline industry. When his noncompete agreement expired, he started JetBlue.

From the beginning, Neeleman recognized the value of the brand. In the book *Flying High*, Neeleman is said to be fond of the concept of "insuring" a customer to a brand, something he learned from research done by the Gallup organization. He explains the concept in the following way: "If people want a cup of coffee, they'll go an extra block to go to Starbucks. They'll walk past three or four coffee houses to go to Starbucks because they like the way they feel about it."[13]

Apparently, people like the way they feel about the JetBlue brand. Just a year after its launch, JetBlue was ranked the number-2 domestic economy airline in the 2001 Zagat Airline Survey. The accolades didn't stop there. JetBlue was voted the number-1 domestic airline in the *Conde Nast Traveler* 2002 Business Traveler Awards, received the 2002 Editor's Choice Award from *Worth* magazine, and was named the number-2 domestic airline in the *Travel and Leisure* 2002 World's Best Awards.

Nothing could make David Neeleman happier since, to him, JetBlue is all about pleasing the Customer. For JetBlue at least, great Customer service has translated into financial success. The airline was profitable in its first year of operation, and in 2002 JetBlue achieved the highest operating margin of any domestic U.S. airline. While the airline business has been extraordinarily challenging of late, JetBlue recorded its 16th consecutive quarter of profitability in Q4 2004. Operating revenues for the quarter were 27 percent higher than Q4 2003, and for the full year, 26.8 percent higher than the previous year.

BUILDING A BILLION-DOLLAR GOLF BUSINESS

Most people might think of the "power players" in golf as the professionals who hit 300-yard-plus drives and win the PGA tournaments. But one of the most powerful people in golf, according to *Golf Digest*, is not a player, but the Chairman of Fortune Brands' Golf business, Wally Uihlein. *Golf Digest* said: "It was once suggested that in the chess game that is the golf industry, Uihlein, 54, is the equivalent of the legendary grandmaster Garry Kasparov."[14]

Uihlein is the brand architect behind golf's first billion-dollar business, the Acushnet Company, consisting of the brands Titleist, FootJoy, Cobra, and Pinnacle. Titleist golf balls and FootJoy golf wear have consistently been the number-1 brands in golf for decades. According to PGA.com, Acushnet's 2004 sales of $1.21 billion make it the only golf equipment company with sales exceeding the billion-dollar mark. This was an increase of 8.1 percent over 2003. According to WebStreet, 2004 net sales for the Titleist brand were nearly $734 million, up 2.4 percent from the previous year, while FootJoy's net sales were over

$294 million, up 11.6 percent. Cobra Golf sales rose 30 percent to over $184 million.

Under Uihlein's direction, Titleist developed entirely new golf ball offerings in 2003, improving the Titleist Pro V1 and the companion Pro V1x. In 2003 champions on the worldwide professional golf tours used Titleist golf balls to achieve 144 victories, more than all other golf balls combined. Uihlein told WebStreet that Titleist was the most played ball worldwide in professional golf by a margin of more than three to one versus any competitor on any tour. FootJoy kept pace that same year with its new DryJoys P.R.O. (Platform Response Outsole) shoes and the new SciFlex golf glove.

In the golf business, being a brand architect is more than driving product innovation and sales. It's also about developing relationships. Uihlein has masterminded relationships with players that have served to ensure his brands' superior image. Numerous leading players endorse Titleist and FootJoy in national advertising.

Over the years, Uihlein has engineered contracts with some of golf's greatest names. There have even been some legendary stories about these deals, such as the story about golfer Moe Norman. According to Jack Kuykendall, owner of the company Natural Golf, Moe Norman was under exclusive contract with Natural Golf when Wally Uihlein asked to meet with him at the 1995 PGA show. During the meeting, Kuykendall said he was interested in helping Moe, not profiting from him. Uihlein said he thought Moe was "one of the four great ball strikers of all times" and, realizing that Moe was hurting financially, suggested paying Moe Norman $5,000 a month for the rest of his life. Kuykendall was delighted with the idea.

When Uihlein proposed the deal to Norman, Norman was skeptical. He told Uihlein he played Titleist balls and wore

FootJoy shoes, but he wanted to know what Uihlein expected of him for the monthly payment. According to Kuykendall, Uihlein said, "You have already done your part, Moe. Titleist is just saying thank you for what you have already done." Kuykendall told Norman he approved of the deal and Moe accepted it. Said Kuykendall: "No company that I know of has ever done an act of appreciation that can parallel what Mr. Uihlein and Titleist did for Moe Norman."[15]

In March 2005, Uihlein was selected to receive The PGA Distinguished Service Award. PGA of America President Roger Warren said of Uihlein: "Golf has been fortunate to have a leader of his caliber, because he believes that there is always a new challenge and a new idea to explore." Wally Uihlein is a great example of a CEO who has a unique brand vision and is himself the ultimate brand champion. He pushes his organization and his agency to deliver breakaway branding ideas quarter after quarter, year after year.

TURNING A FURNITURE STORE INTO "SHOPPERTAINMENT"

Barry and Eliot Tatelman run the ultimate family business. Their grandfather, Samuel, started Jordan's Furniture in 1918 and incorporated the business in 1928. Their father, Edward, joined the business in the late 1930s. During the 1950s and '60s, Barry and Eliot helped out on weekends and during summers—and got hooked.

When they took over the single Jordan's Furniture store in Waltham, Massachusetts, in 1973, perhaps even they couldn't have predicted the wild and crazy ride that would become the modern day Jordan's. Over the next 30-plus years, the brothers would become known to greater Boston residents as "Barry and Eliot," first for their self-produced radio spots, and then for their humorous parodies of other advertisers' television commercials.

But they would become equally renowned for their unique brand of "shoppertainment"—building furniture stores that incorporated, among other things, a Motion Odyssey Movie Ride, a life-size replica of New Orleans' Bourbon Street, and IMAX 3D theaters. Their new Reading, Massachusetts, store features Boston landmarks such as the State House and Public Garden made of jelly beans, a Liquid Fireworks display that erupts every 20 minutes, a trapeze school, and an ice cream shop.

Wait a minute, isn't this supposed to be a furniture store? Well, yes—but it's also a place to be entertained and have fun. Before you think the brothers Tatelman have lost their minds, you might consider the fact that Jordan's is a $250 million business that sells more furniture per square foot than any other furniture retailer in the country.

Barry and Eliot are far more than showmen—they are wise and caring brand architects. In addition to making customers into brand enthusiasts, the brothers treat employees as family, referring to them as the "J-Team." One year, when the staff was smaller, they flew everyone to a Caribbean island as a thank you. The Tatelmans also make a point of giving back to the communities where their stores are located. For example, proceeds from Jordan's Motion Odyssey Movie have been donated to charity, about 50 pieces of product per week go to the Massachusetts Coalition for the Homeless, and nonprofit organizations can use their Natick store's Bourbon Street to hold their fund-raisers.

In 1999 Jordan's was acquired by Berkshire Hathaway, but Barry and Eliot remain as integral parts of the operation. The brothers celebrated the acquisition by rewarding every employee with 50 cents for each hour they had ever worked for Jordan's. Given that many employees stay with Jordan's 10 or 20 years, that was a significant sum. Warren Buffet, CEO of Berkshire Hathaway, said at the time: "Jordan's Furniture is truly one of the most phenomenal and unique companies that I have ever seen. The reputation that Eliot and Barry have earned from their employees, their customers, and the community is unparalleled. This company is a gem!"

The Bottom Line

Perhaps nothing fascinated us more in the development of this book than the increasingly clear realization that behind virtually all breakaway brands existed a brand champion CEO, an empowered CMO or senior marketing executive—and a talented advertising agency who understood them both. This fact isn't talked about or written about much in the world of marketing, but it makes perfect sense. Breakaway branding is *hard*—hard because it takes courage and it requires getting so many elements of the marketing process right. It really isn't surprising this is best done in organizations where there is strong support for branding coming from the very top.

We could go on and on in this chapter if we wanted to and tell stories about more breakaway branding champions. Lou Gerstner, a candidate for best CEO of this generation, used breakaway brand campaigning as a primary weapon in his remarkable turnaround of IBM. Similarly, Jack Welch, another candidate for the CEO Hall of Fame, personally approved every television commercial run by General Electric during his highly successful tenure of more than 20 years at the top of America's most respected corporation. Meg Whitman of eBay, Michael Dell of Dell, and Jim Kilts of Gillette are other top

CEOs known for their belief in the value of breakaway strategy and branding.

As you'll see in Chapter 10, breakaway branding under the guidance of such great CEOs leads to remarkable results—and it's hard to argue with that kind of success.

Chapter 9 Break Points

- THINK ABOUT IT: When you think of a breakaway brand, do you think of a breakaway CEO? Which senior executives are the driving forces behind the world's greatest brands? What role do C-level executives play in marketing your brand or brands?

- Senior management plays a crucial role in the breakaway branding process.

- Ultimately, the breakaway brand's true hero must be the CEO, the COO, or another C-level executive who drives the brand's success.

- CEOs know a brand that stands apart has the potential to drive a company's sales, protect its margins, grow its profitability, and increase its market cap.

- Often it is the CEO or another C-level executive's role to act as a brand visionary.

- When a senior executive adopts the role of brand champion, his or her enthusiasm becomes infectious—and the troops follow the lead.

- A Chief has the opportunity to be the primary architect of the breakaway brand—and when that happens, the possibilities are limitless.

- The role of a great advertising agency is to help its clients' Chiefs tell their story in the most truthful, powerful, integrated manner possible.

CHAPTER 10
Breakaway Results

As we have demonstrated in previous chapters, despite the numerous obstacles that marketers face, breakaway brands *can* be built, in almost any category, on almost any budget. No matter how tough the competition, or how weak the current brand situation, a brilliant marketing team can, with support from C-level executives, find their brand's truth, develop a winning campaign concept, and set out to build a success story. It takes talent, time, and passion—but it is possible.

Hopefully, this book provides you with a better idea of what a breakaway brand looks like, the actions that are required to build one, and what type of results such a brand can deliver for its enterprise.

Which brings us to the focus of this chapter: breakaway brand *results*.

No point in this book is more important than the fact that true breakaway brand marketing campaigns almost always deliver extraordinary results. While it takes a lot of energy, time, talent, and courage to build them, breakaway brand campaigns are well worth the effort.

ABSOLUT, Altoids, Apple, BMW, Citizens Bank, FootJoy, JetBlue, Nike, Royal Caribbean, Target, Titleist, truth, Volkswagen, and the other brands we've written about in this book are all breakaway brands. More important, these brands and their marketing teams have all delivered extraordinary results for their CEOs, their companies, and their shareholders.

The single biggest reason more CEOs should demand breakaway branding campaigns from their organizations and their marketing agencies is because of the positive economic impact such campaigns can deliver. In this chapter, we'll look at the results of ten breakaway brands and hopefully inspire more marketers to reach for the brass ring of becoming the next great break-away brand.

A key point: What you find when you dig into the business and financial results of breakaway brands is that they deliver valuable results for their companies in many more ways than brand managers and their agencies normally discuss. Break-away brand results go far beyond increases in awareness, brand perception, and purchase intent—the traditional measures of marketing success. More thorough and complete measures of brand strength are necessary to fully appreciate the enormous total economic value of breakaway branding.

Breakaway brand results go far beyond increases in awareness, brand perception, and purchase intent—the traditional measures of marketing success. More thorough and complete measures of brand strength are necessary to fully appreciate the enormous value of breakaway branding.

Here is just a partial list of the economic levers of breakaway brand campaigns:

- Increases in brand awareness

- Increases in advertising awareness

- Increases in purchase intent

- Sales gains

- Increased brand loyalty

- Increased margins

- The ability to raise prices (quite possibly the single greatest economic reward of breakaway brands)

- Decreased incentive expenses (in many industries, almost as valuable an outcome as raising prices)

- Strong trade loyalty

- Increased sales force motivation and efficiency

- Improved employee morale (don't laugh—would you rather work at Target or Kmart?)

- Lower employee turnover

- Increased positive press

- Free marketplace "buzz"

- Rising stock price and Price/Earnings ratios

- Increased brand or company valuation

Yes, this is a long and rather eye-opening list of breakaway brand benefits. But when you stop and think about how a campaign at the quality level of "Drivers wanted" brings real value to the enterprise it represents, all of these benefits are true. Marketing and branding leaders like Lou Gerstner, Phil Knight, Steve Jobs, Larry Fish, and Dan Hanrahan intuitively understand this. Unfortunately, too many senior managers who focus exclusively on the financial side do not.

Breakaway Branding at Work: Ten Proof Points

If there is merit to the notion that being a breakaway brand leads to a stellar ROI, then the results achieved by the brand should prove it. Here we highlight ten brands and demonstrate the long-term economic impact of their ability to break away.

1. VOLKSWAGEN

Volkswagen introduced the marketing theme "Drivers wanted" in 1995. In 1998 the company introduced the New Beetle. Allison-Fisher International, one of the leading suppliers of market research to the automotive industry, conducted research on the Volkswagen brand in 2002 to determine the long-term impact of the "Drivers wanted" campaign. The analysis showed the following from 1995 to 2002 for the Volkswagen brand:

- Unaided brand awareness increased 173 percent.

- Brand opinion had favorably increased 73 percent.

- Unaided purchase consideration increased 225 percent.

- Advertising recall increased 119 percent.

"Drivers wanted" became the most recognized tag line in the automobile industry, and Volkswagen advertising campaigns have become among the most awarded for brand awareness, creative excellence, and market impact.

Between 1995 and 2002, U.S. sales of Volkswagen automobiles rose from 115,000 to over 300,000. The number of units sold went up while promotional costs went down. Volkswagen had allocated over $3,000 per car per year for incentives during the early '90s; yet during the late '90s, the promotional cost per car per year was reduced to $1,000 or less. The strength of the brand and the brand's marketing was such that Volkswagens could be sold at higher prices with improved margins. Just think, saving $2,000 in incentive expenses on 300,000 units sold frees up $600,000,000 for increased profits or reinvestment into the business.

As a breakaway brand, Volkswagen could maintain and even raise its prices rather than devalue its cars with price reductions. This is a powerful lesson for brands aspiring to break away.

The breakaway brand, more than any other, can be sold at a premium price and reduce, rather than increase, promotional costs. Why? Because breakaway brands have such strong appeal, so they are not always subject to the same price sensitivity of ordinary brands. Look at Starbucks, Mercedes-Benz, and the Apple iPod when it was first introduced. These brands all enjoy brand status, which allows their prices to be set higher than competitive products.

2. ROYAL CARIBBEAN

In 1999 Royal Caribbean International broke away from its competitors with a new marketing campaign that targeted a more active, adventurous vacation-seeker with the theme "Get out there." This not only repositioned Royal Caribbean—it sent shock waves through the cruise industry. From 2000 to 2004, Royal Caribbean has achieved the following results:

- Unaided brand awareness has increased more than 30 percent.

- Brand preference has increased 30 percent.

- Average daily web traffic has increased 425 percent.

- Online bookings are up over 300 percent.

- Loyalty program enrollment is up 90 percent.

The average age of Royal Caribbean's first-time cruising customer has dropped from 44 years of age in 2000 to 36 years of age in 2004.

"Get out there" remains the theme of Royal Caribbean's marketing strategy and continues to generate breakthrough awareness for the brand today.

The yields of Royal Caribbean Cruises Ltd. ("RCCL," which includes Royal Caribbean International and Celebrity Cruises) have outpaced their primary competitor in 2002, 2003, and the first two quarters of 2004. For 2004 Royal Caribbean reported revenues of $4.6 billion, up 20.4 percent from 2003 revenues of $3.8 billion. Net income for the year of $474.7 million was up from $280.7 million in 2003. RCCL has been rated the "most recommended cruise line by travel agents" according to a number of industry-research studies. Royal Caribbean will end 2005 with some 3 million guests.

The impact of Royal Caribbean's breakaway strategy on its stock price has been equally significant. As shown in Figure 10-1, between September 30, 2001, and December 31, 2004, Royal Caribbean's stock price went up 431 percent, versus the S&P 500, which rose 14 percent during that same time period.

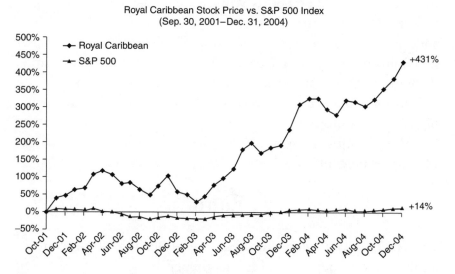

Figure 10-1 Royal Caribbean's stock has appreciated in value more than 400 percent from September 2001 through December 2004.

3. TITLEIST AND FOOTJOY

Titleist is and has remained the number-1 golf ball brand for decades. FootJoy is and has remained the number-1 golf shoe brand.

Growth hasn't come easy in a market that analysts say is mature. In 2003, for example, rounds of golf played in the U.S. declined 3 percent, but sales of Fortune Brands' golf brands increased 11 percent.[1] The Acushnet Company, a division of Fortune Brands, is golf's first and only billion-dollar business, encompassing the brands Titleist, FootJoy, Cobra, and Pinnacle. Acushnet's 2004 sales were $1.21 billion, an increase of 8.1 percent over 2003. Of that amount, Titleist brand sales were nearly $734 million while FootJoy's net sales were over $294 million. Cobra Golf sales rose to over $184 million. In the first quarter of 2005, Acushnet's sales increased to a record $342.6 million, with earnings increasing 11 percent to $56.7 million.[2]

In June 2003, Top-Flite Golf Company filed for bankruptcy. Formerly part of Spalding Sports Worldwide, Top-Flite produced golf balls that were a primary competitor to Titleist golf balls. Callaway, another golf company, acquired Top-Flite's assets in September 2003. From 2000 through 2003, Titleist continued to gain market share even as Top-Flite's market share dramatically declined.

FootJoy launched an advertising campaign in 1999 featuring SignBoy, a humorous fictional character. Since the inception of SignBoy, FootJoy has seen record sales and market share increases of over 10 percent.

4. TRUTH

The facts about teen smoking are sobering: 90 percent of adult smokers begin smoking at or before age 19; 95 percent of teens who smoke cigarettes start before age 16; between

30 and 50 percent of youth who try a cigarette will become daily smokers; each day, more than 2,000 children and teens become regular smokers—about 800,000 each year. One third of children and teen regular smokers will eventually die from a tobacco-related disease.

That's why, in early 2000, the American Legacy Foundation launched truth, the antismoking campaign targeting children and teens. Soon after truth's launch, Monitoring the Future, one of the nation's most comprehensive substance abuse-surveys, cited the truth campaign in explaining the sharp decline in cigarette smoking among 8th, 10th, and 12th graders. By the fall of that year, truth's awareness among children aged 12 to 17 was well over 50 percent. In 2001, teens voted truth one of the top three advertising campaigns (the other two were Budweiser and Volkswagen).[3] By spring 2002, about two years after its introduction, truth's awareness among the 12 to 17 age group rose to over 50 percent. Within this age group, 92 percent said truth gave good reasons not to smoke.[4]

A recent study showed a decline in youth smoking prevalence among all students in grades 8, 10, and 12 from over 25 percent to 18 percent between 1999 and 2002. The study also found that the truth campaign accounted for about 22 percent of this decline.[5]

truth has had a major, measurable long-term impact as an antismoking campaign:

- Seventy-five percent of all 12- to 17-year-olds in the nation (21 million) can accurately describe one or more of the truth ads.

- Nearly 90 percent of youths aged 12 to 17 (25 million) said the truth ad they saw was convincing.

- Eighty-five percent (24 million) said the truth ad gave them good reasons not to smoke.

- More than 300,000 young lives have been saved by this highly effective breakaway brand.

5. CITIZENS BANK

When Citizens Bank began its new brand advertising in 2001, featuring legendary service ads under the theme "Not your typical bank," the bank holding company was the 28th largest bank in the country. Citizens Bank had 370 branches in four New England states.

Today, after several acquisitions and a continuing emphasis on differentiating the brand, Citizens Bank is a $132 billion commercial bank holding company, the eighth largest commercial banking company in the country ranked by deposits. Citizens has more than 1,600 offices and 25,000 employees in 13 states throughout New England, the Mid-Atlantic, and the Midwest.

In 2003 Citizens acquired Cambridgeport Bank and Community National Bank in Massachusetts and Commonwealth Bancorp in Pennsylvania. The following year, Citizens acquired Roxborough-Manayunk Bank in Pennsylvania and Charter One Financial in Ohio.

Citizens was the number-1 U.S. Small Business Administration lender in both the Mid-Atlantic and New England regions, and number 2 in the nation, in 2002 and 2003. Citizens Bank had total assets of $78 billion in January 2004, with asset quality ranked among the best of the top 20 U.S. banks at the end of 2003.

For the year 2004, Citizens had record pretax contributions of $1.90 billion, up 36 percent from $1.40 billion for 2003—its 12th consecutive year of record results.

6. NIKE

The Nike "Just do it" campaign launched in 1988, and it seems from that point on, Nike never looked back. Nike has been one of the biggest brand marketing success stories ever.

The long-term economic impact of the Nike brand is unquestionable. One interesting way to view Nike's success is in comparison to its major rival, Reebok. Nike and Reebok have very similar product lines. But the gap between Nike as a breakaway brand and its competitor is significant. Marketing has made all the difference.

Reebok has marketed aggressively at times, but the company has not achieved the same consistency or super-status of Nike. If we compared Nike and Reebok to world-class marathon runners, Reebok always seems to finish in second place. Nike's ability to run a sustainable race and win the sales marathon year after year is simply not to be questioned.

As illustrated in Figure 10-2, from 1994 to 2004, Nike's sales grew from $3.9 billion to $12.3 billion, an increase of about 265 percent. Reebok's sales went from $2.9 billion to $3.8 billion, an increase of about 30 percent. During the same period, Nike's profit rose 159 percent, from $365 million to $946 million, while Reebok's profit decreased 14 percent, from $223 million to $192 million.

Nike's stock price increased 27 percent for fiscal year 2004 and the company raised its dividend 40 percent during the year. For the third quarter of its fiscal year 2005, ending February 28, 2005, Nike's revenues increased 14 percent to $3.3 billion, versus $2.9 billion for the same period in the prior year.

While Nike's dominance has been virtually unchallenged until now, the competitive environment is about to undergo a dramatic change. In August 2005, Adidas announced it would purchase Reebok, combining Nike's two largest competitors.

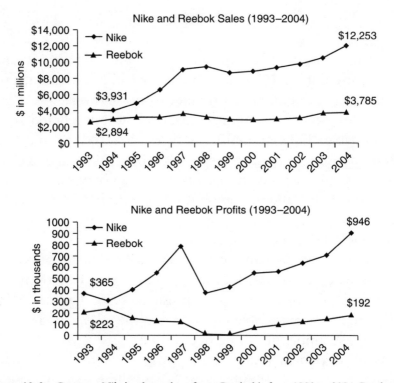

Figure 10-2 Compare Nike's sales and profits to Reebok's from 1993 to 2004. Breakaway brand Nike easily outdistances its major competitor.

7. APPLE

With the launch of the iPod brand, Apple once again became the breakaway brand it was in earlier years. *The Wall Street Journal* described it this way: "Apple Computer Inc., riding one of the most dramatic revivals in its turbulent history, said its fiscal first-quarter profit more than quadrupled on a 74% increase in sales, reflecting strong demand during the holidays for its iPod portable music player and Macintosh computers."[6]

Clearly the iPod and its associated digital music software, iTunes, played a major role in driving Apple's success, but Apple continued its brand innovation by introducing a $99 iPod and a

$499 Mac computer in early 2005. The buzz for Apple was all positive, as its stock became 2004's hottest property and analysts predicted a rosy future. Apple announced a two–for–one stock split in February 2005.

Apple ended its 2004 fiscal year with $9.7 billion in sales. For its fiscal 2005 second quarter ending in March 2005, Apple posted a net profit of $290 million compared to a net profit of $46 million at the same time a year ago. The company reported revenue increases of 70 percent and net income increases of over 500 percent year-over-year. During the quarter, Apple shipped over 1 million Macintosh units, and over five times as many iPods—5.3 million. For its fiscal third quarter 2005, Apple's net was $320 million. Apple's status as a breakaway brand was only enhanced by Brandchannel.com's *2004 Readers' Choice Awards*, in which Apple was voted the number-1 global brand by almost 2,000 readers from 75 countries.

While the iPod isn't the only reason for Apple's resurgence, it is a major one. iPod is a great example of the role a hero product can play in building breakaway brand value. Without a breakaway brand like iPod, it is unlikely Apple would have achieved the dramatic rise in stock price, keyed almost precisely to iPod's emergence. In the graph in Figure 10-3, you'll notice that Apple's stock price spikes from about September 2004 through the end of the calendar year. This contributes to a rise in stock value over a two-year period of 497 percent, compared to the S&P 500, which rose 43 percent during the same period.

8. ALTOIDS

Altoids, the quirky British breath confection, has turned the breath mint category into a competitive, thriving market. London confectionary firm Smith & Company changed the packaging of Altoids from cardboard to metal tins during the 1920s, and at the

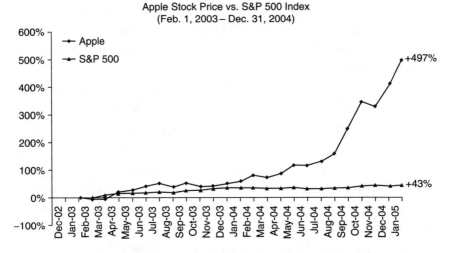

Figure 10-3 Apple's stock price increased sharply about the time of the iPod introduction. Between 2003 and 2005, the stock's value went up almost 500 percent.

same time labeled the mint "curiously strong." That would be the beginning of a breakaway brand. But Altoids' rise to fame in the U.S. wasn't easy—the mint had a small but cult-like following among young and active adults when it arrived in America. Ranked sixth in the U.S. mint category in 1995, Altoids was priced three times higher than the competition. It had limited distribution, low brand awareness, and no advertising.

Advertising agency Leo Burnett had a small ad budget to work with and decided to introduce the brand in 12 city areas where Altoids had strong distribution. Relying on nontraditional advertising that included such tactics as billboards, posters placed on the sides of buildings, transit shelters, bus wraps, and telephone kiosks, the agency created a campaign with a vintage, out-of-the-ordinary feeling.

The campaign produced startling results: unaided brand awareness rose by 60 percent and regular usage increased 36 percent. Volume was up over 50 percent in the 12 city areas. Since Altoids began advertising in 1995, its U.S. consumption has increased by a cumulative 500 percent. Today, Altoids is the number-1 breath mint in America.

In November 2004, Kraft announced it would sell the Altoids brand, along with Life Savers and other smaller brands, to the Wm. Wrigley, Jr., Company for about $1.48 billion. Wrigley, itself a leader in chewing gum, will no doubt find continued success in its newly acquired breakaway brand.

9. TARGET

The discount retail store category was born in 1962, when Wal-Mart, Kmart, and Target all opened their doors. While Wal-Mart began to dominate in the 1980s with a low-price strategy and ultimately became the undisputed category leader, Target made a conscious effort to differentiate itself, becoming an innovator in "cheap chic." Target's concept was upscale discounting and bringing design and fashion to the masses. Target went on to secure partnerships with high-end designers, and to sell more upscale brands at a discount than its rivals.

In the 1990s, Target advertising resembled a fashion brand more than it did a retailer. Equally important, Target created a strong, memorable, breakaway brand by consistently relying on its bold red color and signature bull's-eye logo in everything from ads to newspaper inserts to store signage and product labeling. Target also became a leader in interruptive, buzz marketing—pioneering the use of "pop-up stores" and creating industry breakthrough promotions, such as its "wake up call" campaign featuring celebrities who "called" consumers via a recorded message on the day after Thanksgiving.

In the past ten years, at a time when retail bankruptcies have boomed more than retail sales, Target Corporation has approximately doubled its number of stores, roughly tripled its revenues, and more than quadrupled its pretax segment profit, according to the company. Sales exceeded $48 billion in 2004, making Target the number-2 general merchandiser in the U.S., behind Wal-Mart. Between 1997 and 2004, sales for Target Corporation rose 70 percent, at a compound annual growth rate of 8 percent.[7] Today there are over 1,300 Target stores in the U.S. Ninety-six percent of American consumers recognize the Target bull's-eye.

10. IBM

While we didn't really address IBM earlier in this book, a strong case can be made for the company's status as a breakaway brand during "the Lou Gerstner years." Gerstner was CEO from 1993 until March 2002. He was legendary for raising "Big Blue" out of its financial doldrums and turning the brand around. Gerstner restructured the company and created a common vision, rejecting the notion of breaking IBM into several operating units. In his book on the rise, fall, and rebirth of IBM, Gerstner explains: "I turned my attention to three areas that, if not fundamentally changed, would disable any hope of a strategy built around integration—organization, brand image, and compensation."[8]

Gerstner devotes an entire chapter in his book to "reviving the brand." During his tenure, Gerstner focused considerable attention on the company's brand image. IBM consolidated many advertising agencies to one global agency, Ogilvy & Mather, leading to IBM's ability to find its brand voice and become a true integrated marketer. For example, IBM was the first company to capitalize on the e-business trend, creating a symbol with a stylized "e" and coordinating a major traditional and online campaign around it. By coining the term "e-business," IBM defined a category and became associated

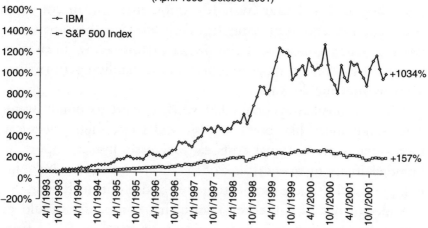

IBM Stock vs. S&P 500 Index
(April. 1993–October 2001)

Figure 10-4 The "Gerstner Years" were good for IBM's stock—during this period when IBM was a breakaway brand, IBM's stock appreciated over 1000 percent.

with it as a market leader—despite initially ranking low as a provider in this space.

The result of Gerstner's efforts, and IBM's brand revival, was a dramatic uptick in the company's financial health. IBM's sales had slipped prior to Gerstner's arrival, sliding from $64.5 billion in 1992 to $62.7 billion in 1993. But from 1993 to 2001, the "Gerstner years," sales rose from $62.7 billion to $85.9 billion, an increase of over 135 percent. As shown in Figure 10-4, between April 1993 and October 2001, IBM's stock price rose 1034 percent, as compared to the S&P 500, which rose 157 percent.

Breakaway Branding Works

Our objective in this chapter was to demonstrate with brief yet compelling examples how extraordinary results can be returned by breakaway brands and the leadership teams that develop them.

Breakaway brands outperform their competitors on individual measures, such as brand awareness gains, increases in consideration, and perception of value. But their *true* value becomes crystal clear when you look at the bigger picture—how breakaway brands multiply success because of their outstanding performance in many measurable ways.

When a breakaway brand has worked hard to build awareness, uniqueness, likeability, loyalty, and trust, then prices can increase and promotional costs can decrease. Just as important, brand elasticity increases (think of the diverse categories Nike has conquered). Put these factors together, and profits truly soar.

Superior results is the key reason that companies should be demanding breakaway brand–quality marketing programs from their in-house marketing leaders, as well as from their outside partner agencies. Breakaway branding is where the money is. In today's highly competitive business landscape, building a breakaway brand may be one of the few remaining ways a company that markets branded products and services can succeed.

Chapter 10 Break Points

- THINK ABOUT IT: What are some of the measurement criteria you would use to determine the success of a brand's marketing program? How would you assess the ROI of building a breakaway brand?

- Despite numerous obstacles that marketers face, breakaway brands can be built, in almost any category, on almost any budget.

- No point in this book is more important than the fact that true breakaway brand marketing campaigns almost always deliver extraordinary results.

- The single biggest reason more CEOs should demand breakaway branding campaigns from their organizations and their marketing agencies is because of the positive economic impact they are guaranteed to deliver.

- What you find when you dig into the business and financial results of breakaway brands is that they deliver valuable results for their companies in many more ways than brand managers and their agencies normally discuss.

- When a breakaway brand has worked hard to build awareness, uniqueness, likeability, loyalty, and trust, then prices can increase and promotional costs can decrease.

- Superior results is the key reason that companies should be demanding breakaway brand-quality marketing programs.

CHAPTER 11

Breakaway Branding in Business—and Beyond

Our goal in this book was to tell the story of breakaway brands, to discuss some of their secrets to success, and to honor a few of the highly effective marketing and business leaders who embrace a breakaway style of branding.

They're pretty compelling stories, when you stop to think about it. The breakaway brands we've showcased are not only highly successful, but they are also talked about, admired, awarded—and fun to be involved with. Yes, breakaway brands require lots of hard work, vision, and guts. But the results clearly seem to justify the effort.

What's fascinating to us—and somewhat troubling—is that so few marketers actually build brands and marketing campaigns of breakaway quality. According to *Advertising Age*, U.S. companies invest around $950 in advertising for every person in the country. Some $280 *billion* per year is spent marketing brands to the American public.[1] Despite this, the number of brands that are truly differentiated is alarmingly low. Too many marketing teams at companies, and their partner agencies, will settle for undifferentiated brand positioning, less than spectacular creative approaches, flawed integration strategies, or a total lack of brand consistency from marketing element to element, or from one year's campaign to the next.

What's fascinating to us—and somewhat troubling—is that so few marketers actually build brands and marketing campaigns of breakaway quality.

Even more troubling is the fact that CEOs who are not brand champions will accept this type of me-too, inferior marketing as the norm. No wonder many CEOs devalue marketing and underfund it in their organizations.

We simply believe the world needs—and consumers deserve—more breakaway brand success stories. This would help smart companies better grow their sales, profits, and company valuation. This could help CMOs keep their jobs far longer than the 24-month average we've read is typical. Consumers would see more intelligent, aspirational advertising when they sit down to watch television, work at their computers, or open that stack of low, low-interest-rate credit card mailings every month. (It certainly brings a whole new meaning to "low interest.") And maybe more advertising agencies might obtain that place at the branding leadership table that they so passionately desire.

Interestingly, breakaway branding is at the heart of how you win in the world. It is inextricably linked with the American dream. Breakaway brands win in business. Breakaway brand gurus rise to the top of their fields, whether it's a CEO like Steve Jobs, a CMO like Theresa McLaughlin, or a SVP like Dan Hanrahan—or an ad agency partner like Arnold Worldwide, TBWA\Chiat\Day, or Crispin Porter + Bogusky.

The same holds true of those who break away and become successful in almost every competitive arena. Ivy League schools separate themselves from their competitors and enjoy decades of prosperity. The Boston Red Sox turn year after year of heart-breaking losses into a category-of-one Major League Baseball brand; even before the 2004 World Series win, the Sox franchise value was approaching $1 billion. In politics, the revered names of Washington, Jefferson, Lincoln, Kennedy, Reagan, and Clinton represent striking examples of breakaway brands.

The reality is that these "brands," like their breakaway product brethren, make it big in America by taking risks and breaking away from their competitors, not by playing it safe and imitating others.

Ten Rules for Success: Building a Breakaway Brand

To build more breakaway brands, brand development leaders must first take a hard look at their current brands and their brand building process. Are the brands *breakaway* brands? Is there a breakaway vision in place to get there? Does the company's process allow a breakaway brand to be born and nurtured over the three to five years it takes to build a truly great brand success story?

This is a critical conversation every company that invests significantly in marketing should have on an annual basis. Every stakeholder must ask: What kind of marketer do we *really* want to be? Every marketing team should force the conversation. Every CEO should encourage the conversation to take place. Every board of directors should *care* whether breakaway brands are being built—or whether it's just business as usual. Business as usual generally isn't good enough in today's overbranded, ultra-competitive, media-fragmented marketing environment.

---

*Every stakeholder must ask: What kind of marketer do we **really** want to be?*

Your advertising agency should participate in that conversation. Talented, successful advertising agencies can play an important role in the breakaway branding process. No client wants to do bad work. No client wants to receive a lower return on their advertising investment if a higher ROI approach is offered up. Great agencies understand the value of breakaway branding. They have their own best-case histories, and they have access to others that are highly relevant to their clients' brands and challenges. Every agency owes its clients a thoughtful, provocative, convincing conversation about building better brands and fostering breakaway brand thinking.

Only when a smart client and a talented agency embrace this critical conversation can the team begin to build a breakaway brand success story. And that's when they can apply these ten rules for success.

Building a breakaway brand takes hard work, guts, and creativity. And sometimes it means taking risks and making sacrifices. But as you've seen throughout this book, the brand that stands out, the brand that breaks away, achieves extraordinary results. Here, then, are ten rules for success in building a breakaway brand.

1. MAKE A COMMITMENT

Your entire organization, from the top down, needs to make a commitment to build and support a breakaway brand. The process starts with your company's corporate brand and your product brands. Take a hard look at your existing brands and assess whether they are me-too look-alikes, or whether they have truly differentiating and distinguishing characteristics that can be leveraged to create a category of one. Get your company behind developing new products that have breakaway attributes. Create a marketing program that dramatizes your unique product advantages and separates you in the marketplace.

2. GET A "CHIEF" BEHIND IT

Few breakaway branding initiatives have a chance of success without the enthusiastic support of your CEO, COO, or CMO. A senior executive at your company must play the role of brand visionary, brand champion, and brand architect. The Chief's support must be communicated throughout every level of your organization so the troops follow the lead. Commitment to the brand and what it stands for should be evident at the most senior levels—even the board of directors. Picking the right partner agency and getting the agency's chiefs fired up about your business is just as important.

3. FIND YOUR BRAND TRUTH

Ultimately, the DNA of your breakaway brand is its brand truth. It is what defines and differentiates every breakaway brand. The brand truth can inform every other decision you have to make. It is the single most important weapon a brand will ever have in the battle for increased awareness, profitability, market share, and even share price. To get to the brand truth, your brand must go through a process. Typically, the process involves understanding your company's vision, gaining business insight into your competitors and market conditions, developing target insight into your market and audience, finding a winning mindset for your product, and then finding the product's brand truth—fundamentally, what the brand stands for and represents to the winning mindset.

4. TARGET A WINNING MINDSET

The winning mindset is the potent, aspirational, shared "view of life" amongst all core audience segments. It reveals to you how best to match your company's vision and your product with the right target audience. The winning mindset becomes the filter through which all of your advertising and promotional activities should flow. If you understand and embrace the winning mindset, you can clearly define the messaging and communications that targets the winning mindset.

5. CREATE A CATEGORY OF ONE

To build a breakaway brand, your brand needs to stand apart from others in its own category. Ideally, it should stand out as a model brand that transcends categories. Your brand needs to open a defining gap between itself and its competitors—whether it is new to the market or an existing player. Then your breakaway brand becomes a category of one—redefining its category so it stands apart from its competitors.

6. DEMAND A GREAT CAMPAIGN

Great campaigns are a team sport—they require a partnership between you and your agency to create a campaign that breaks away. Never compromise on a campaign, because without a great campaign, your breakaway brand can fizzle. If your brand is new, a campaign introduces it to the public. For an existing product, a campaign can renew interest and rejuvenate sales. A campaign uses a combination of coordinated, integrated media to capture the brand essence of a product, generate awareness among the right target audiences, and create demand. Every element of a breakaway campaign should be carefully orchestrated to play off the other, and each element must ultimately support the brand and the brand promise. A breakaway campaign stands out in the crowd, because it cuts through the clutter, resonates with the consumer, and differentiates the brand from all of its competitors.

While the tactics may change, the underlying strategy and message of a breakaway campaign often remains for many years.

7. TIRELESSLY INTEGRATE

You shouldn't rely on a single medium to launch a new brand or promote an existing brand—integration is the name of the game. The marketing world is changing rapidly, and your brand marketing needs to change with it. According to one recent study, viewers will be able to skip over 10 percent of U.S. television advertisements by 2009 because of growing digital video recorder technology.[2] That means you have to integrate many media to spread your risk and effectively reach your target audience. Depending on the audience you're trying to reach, your campaign might integrate both network and cable TV, print and online advertising, direct mail, e-mail, radio, and often nontraditional media—everything from street marketing to publicity stunts to contests that may appear on the product packaging itself. Breakaway brands tend to have very well-integrated campaigns—the strategy, messaging, and look and feel are carried successfully from one medium to another to gain maximum impact. It isn't easy to integrate—but it's never been more essential.

8. TAKE RISKS

Today, 80 percent of brands are merely treading water in a sea of gray. Only 20 percent are making waves. You can't afford to have your product sink in the sea—and that may mean taking a calculated risk or two—or three—to ensure your brand rises above the others. It takes more than money alone to create a separate and distinctly different brand. Launching a brand or growing market share requires an aggressive and potentially risky brand-building and marketing strategy. Brands that separate from their competition amaze and delight consumers. In some cases, breakaway brands start entirely new categories. Whatever it takes, don't be afraid to take risks.

9. ACCELERATE NEW PRODUCT DEVELOPMENT

Nothing is more important than differentiating a product in the marketplace—but the only way to rise above me-too branding is to innovate and do something different and unique with the product. It may mean throwing away an old product brand and reinventing it. Or it may mean starting from scratch. A breakaway product could be a first mover in an established category, a product so strong it dominates a category, or the creator of an entirely new category. The product itself must have outstanding attributes. It should embody smart positioning, innovation, an audience connection, leadership, and, above all, a brand truth that is *true* to the brand. If you are committed to breakaway branding, you may find that you will need to have a constant stream of new products available to execute against your vision over time.

10. INVEST AS IF YOUR BRAND DEPENDS ON IT

Building a breakaway brand is serious business, so it takes a serious business investment. You need to invest in the product, of course—but you should also invest adequately in the product packaging and a smart integrated marketing campaign to get the biggest bang for your buck. As you've seen in this book, even small brands can make a distinctive splash, and clever marketing that breaks through doesn't always have to cost a lot of money. Nonetheless, breakaway brands that are underfunded could get lost in an overcrowded marketplace, no matter how great they are. So invest wisely…as if your brand depends on it.

Breakaway Branding Is Championship Branding

You've probably figured out by now that to build a breakaway brand, you must do many things well. Take another look at the ten steps outlined above. Brand marketers might execute six, seven, or even eight of these steps and still fail just as miserably as someone who does none of them. That's because the organizations and leaders behind breakaway brands take *all* of these steps, and more. They do so many things right.

Builders of breakaway brands are true champions. What Apple, Nike, Royal Caribbean, Titleist, and Dell accomplish in their competitive arena is analogous to what great teams like the NFL's New England Patriots have done in their arena. They've won three of the last four Super Bowls, not because they do one thing or several things well—they do many, many things well. The Pats are lauded for being a great team with visionary leadership at the top and smart players who execute well at every position and have a true passion for playing the game and *winning*. The Patriots don't necessarily do any one thing better than anyone else (although we are huge Tom Brady fans). In fact, they do everything well in a relentlessly integrated manner.

This football championship formula is not unlike the formula companies use to develop breakaway brands: strong leadership at the top, a clear vision, flawless execution of branding elements, excellent integration, and a passion to win year after year. That pretty much describes what it takes to build a breakaway brand.

Strong leadership at the top, a clear vision, flawless execution of branding elements, excellent integration, and a passion to win year after year. That pretty much describes what it takes to build a breakaway brand.

BREAKAWAY BRANDING IS A TEAM SPORT

Not surprisingly, breakaway branding is a team sport—in business, it may be the ultimate team sport. Within the Volkswagen, Mercedes-Benz, MasterCard, Jack Daniels, and Starbucks success stories, you'll find a striking similarity, as with most breakaway brands: there is a strong leader working with a core marketing group, surrounded by a larger marketing machine, probably joined at the hip with a highly creative advertising agency that shares the vision of the leader. These kinds of teams work well together, month after month, year after year, to turn a good brand concept into a breakaway branding success story.

This points to a key reason why many clients never achieve the branding success they desire. Without building a team engineered for breakaway branding, it will be difficult to succeed. It isn't easy to find a great branding team leader—but behind every breakaway brand is a passionate champion who truly has the talent, leadership skills, creative sensibility, and guts to build a winning brand. This could be a CEO, CMO, or a senior VP of marketing, but every successful team has an inspiring leader. He or she then must build a winning team, and they in turn must find the agency they trust with their brand's future.

A great example of this is the executive team at Procter & Gamble, A. G. Lafley, President and CEO, and Jim Stengel, Global Marketing Officer. While many consider P&G one of the greatest brand-builders on the planet, ordinary brand marketing just isn't good enough for this branding duo. Lafley has refocused the company on its core brands, while Stengel has urged advertisers and their agencies to develop better measurement research and ROI models. Stengel has also streamlined P&G's agency and media buying relationships.

A great agency partner who can develop a strong creative position is critical in building breakaway brands as well. Without the right core creative concept (think "Just do it" for Nike or "Drivers wanted" for Volkswagen), the relentless integration and multiyear consistency required to break away is hard to achieve. Unfortunately, too many clients never build the team or find the core creative concept they need to develop a breakaway brand.

DON'T OVER-TEST THE BREAKAWAY BRAND

Another destroyer of breakaway brand momentum is relying too much on testing, particularly the traditional standardized testing of day after recall. While most breakaway brands measure carefully and use data extensively, few rely exclusively on creative testing measures to determine their creative development plans.

Many companies greatly admire the work of brands like Nike, Apple, Volkswagen, and MINI (as well they should), yet when they go searching for a new campaign or a new agency, they insist on putting the work they like through their traditional testing process. One definition of insanity is "doing things the way they have always been done, while seeking a radically improved outcome." Trying to achieve Nike-quality work using the black-box testing techniques designed to create Mr. Whipple or the Planters Peanut Man is insanity.

Breakaway brands are modern brands that mix rational selling with making emotional connections in a highly relevant and aspirational manner. This modern breakaway branding formula is very different from the classic packaged-goods formula of thirty years ago. To do more modern work, clients must embrace more modern marketing approaches and employ creative talent in tune with today's more casual, fast-paced, multicultural, and irreverent world.

Any Brand Can Become a Breakaway Brand

One interesting finding in our research for this book is that almost any brand, in any category, and on any budget, can become a breakaway brand. What it takes to be successful is *a desire to break away* and *a relentless commitment to be different.* New brands can break away quickly when they do the right things. Snapple juice, Gatorade sports drink, and Red Bull energy drink revolutionized their respective beverage categories. ABSOLUT turned the vodka business around 20 years ago, and Grey Goose has spun it yet again over the past five. Smartfoods put snacks in black bags supported by a crazy small-space advertising campaign with amazing results. Altoids packaged its way to success even though it was more expensive than its competitors and had a small advertising budget. Crest Whitestrips targeted relatively narrow markets like brides and gay men to quickly build a very large new brand extension for P&G. Silk soy milk and the airline JetBlue are great examples of newer breakaway brands that have made a big impact without giant marketing budgets.

More mature brands can be reenergized with breakaway brand thinking, as well. Steve Jobs almost instantly reignited Apple's brand and business growth with the "Think Different" campaign and his breakaway brand leadership style. Then iPod made Apple a youthful breakaway brand all over again. Volkswagen was one or two bad years away from exiting the ultra-competitive North American market in 1994 before the "Drivers wanted" positioning and campaign helped Americans rediscover the joys of driving VW's uniquely German-engineered, affordable driving machines. Royal Caribbean used new ships and a relentless breakaway branding approach to attract a new kind of passenger, shaking up the entire cruise industry at the same time. IBM's modern, integrated e-business campaign clearly helped adrenalize a formerly fading brand to create a revitalized dominant marketing organization.

Almost any brand, in any category and on any budget, can be a breakaway brand. What it takes to be successful is a desire to break away and a relentless commitment to be different.

Even smaller brands buried behind bigger, stronger competitors can benefit from breakaway brand thinking. In fact, distant challenger brands need breakaway brand thinking the most. Often they lack the funding and the attention needed to regain market momentum without an infusion of radical, fresh thinking. Subway, Lee Jeans, Miller High Life, and Las Vegas are good examples of brands that languished for years but have recently found their brand truths and executed powerful core creative campaigns. With more aggressive leadership and breakaway brand continuity, they are fighting their way back to prominence again very successfully. Las Vegas, for example, attracted a record-breaking 37.4 million visitors in 2004.[3] That growth is largely attributed to the Vegas advertising campaign, "What Happens Here, Stays Here."

The CEO of the Las Vegas Convention and Visitors Authority and the CEO of their agency R&R Partners were the joint recipients of *Brandweek* magazine's 2004 Grand Marketer of the Year award for the campaign's outstanding success.

Money is not the biggest issue in breakaway branding. Attitude, talent, and determination are much more important factors.

BREAKAWAY BRANDING BEYOND BUSINESS

As we briefly mentioned before, the breakaway branding concept extends rather effortlessly into many areas of modern life beyond business brands. In almost any sector of life, particularly here in fame-crazed America, it is the talented individuals and breakaway brands that achieve the greatest success.

Schools are a terrific example of breakaway branding. On the one hand, all of the Ivy League colleges are breakaway brands in and of themselves, reaping the rewards of being famous, differentiated, highly desirable institutions. Yet within the Ivys, Harvard is different from Yale (which is totally different from Princeton) than the three leading fast food or cell phone brands will ever be from each other. Schools seem to get breakaway branding naturally. From their names to their beloved mascots to their sports teams to their unique course offerings, every successful school is unique and well branded.

Celebrities, rock stars, actors, and politicians are themselves breakaway brands. Close your eyes and think about the name John Fitzgerald Kennedy. What a rich brand comes to mind! President Kennedy was unique. From his name to his initials to his heritage, his sailboat, his famous accent, his hair, his youthful exuberance, and his rocking chair, Kennedy naturally built a unique, appealing breakaway brand.

Think Madonna, Arnold Schwarzenegger, The Rolling Stones, The Boston Red Sox, Tiger Woods, Jack Welch. To make it to the top in America, whether as a commercial brand or a celebrity or even a business leader, you have to take a stand on who you are, what makes you unique, and why people might care. You have to break away. While this takes some guts, it clearly is essential if you want to get noticed and to build a customer base or a following of any kind. After all, America itself is a breakaway brand—possibly the greatest example of breakaway branding in our planet's history.[4]

To make it to the top in America, whether as a commercial brand or a celebrity or even a business leader, you have to take a stand on who you are, what makes you unique, and why people might care. You have to break away.

IN THE END, BREAKAWAY BRANDING IS UP TO YOU

We started this book by asking some important questions:

- Why don't more brands break away?

- Why are the majority of brands "me-too," look-alike products?

- Why aren't more brands like Nike in athletic wear, Apple in computers and consumer electronics, BMW and Volkswagen in autos, Altoids in confections, Budweiser in beer, JetBlue in airlines, Royal Caribbean in cruises?

- Why don't more brands invest in memorable advertising campaigns, smartly integrated media, and strategic plans that last for more than five years?

- Why don't more CEOs *demand* that their brands break away?

- Why is the passion gone?

We hope the examples cited in this book will inspire you to bring a new breakaway brand to market, or reinvent an existing brand and turn it into a breakaway brand.

We also hope this book is a call to action.

Let's band together and do away with me-too, look-alike brands. Too many brands in the marketplace are simply knock-offs of others instead of being unique and different. Not enough brands stand out. Not enough brands amaze and delight consumers. Even the increase in company merger activity leads to the disappearance of well-known, long-lasting company and product brands. That's a tragedy.

Building and promoting a breakaway brand is only made more difficult by the new marketing landscape that requires a different approach to brand marketing. To get your brand noticed, you have to integrate media better than ever before. And you may have to do things to get your brand noticed that you've never done before. Today, the consumer is calling the shots. That can humble a brand marketer pretty quickly.

These marketplace factors can be terrifying if you're a risk-averse brand marketer. But if you're a breakaway brand marketer, such factors present you with an unparalleled opportunity. An opportunity to make *your* brand—whether it's a product or service—a breakaway brand.

Study the examples in this book. Follow the strategies and tactics. Separate your brand from the competition. Stand out in an overcrowded marketplace. Apply the principles of breakaway branding...and you might turn a sea of gray into a sea of gold. The benefits of building a breakaway brand are worth the effort. Just do it!

> ### *Building the Breakaway Brand Is a Continuous Process...*
>
> ...so we've created a companion web site to this book. Visit
> www.thebreakawaybrand.com
> to get updates on breakaway brands, learn more about breakaway
> branding, and share your thoughts with us.

Chapter 11 Break Points

Ten rules for success:

1. Make a commitment.

2. Get a "Chief" behind it.

3. Find your brand truth.

4. Target a winning mindset.

5. Create a category of one.

6. Demand a great campaign.

7. Tirelessly integrate.

8. Take risks.

9. Accelerate new product development.

10. Invest as if your brand depends on it.

Endnotes

CHAPTER 1

1. Copernicus Marketing web site (www.copernicusmarketing.com).

2. Mintel International Group web site (www.mintel.com).

3. Productscan Online web site (www.productscan.com).

4. Harumi Ito, Department of Economics, Brown University, Providence, RI, and Darin Lee, LECG, LLC, Cambridge, MA, "Low Cost Carrier Growth in the U.S. Airline Industry: Past, Present, and Future," April 9, 2003.

CHAPTER 2

1. "The 100 Top Brands," *BusinessWeek*, August 1, 2005. *BusinessWeek* works with brand consultant Interbrand to assess the value of a brand using the following information: overall sales and net earnings, isolating earnings generated by the brand from intangibles, projecting future brand earnings on the basis of such factors as market leadership, and geographic reach.

2. Dawn Anfuso, "Simon Says," *iMediaConnection.com*, March 29, 2004 (www.imediaconnection.com/content/3122.asp).

3. Laura M. Holson, "No Golden Years Yet for a 75-Year-Old Mouse," *The New York Times*, November 24, 2003.

4. Anne Saunders, "Seizing the In-Store Experience to Build Brand Value" (speech, Boston Ad Club Symposium, March 9, 2005).

5. Stuart Elliott, "Coffee Liqueur Marketing Heats Up," *The New York Times*, March 29, 2005.

CHAPTER 3

1. Keith Naughton and Bill Vlasic, "The Nostalgia Boom: Why the old is new again," *BusinessWeek*, March 23, 1998.

2. Lawrence K. Fish, "Top to Bottom Branding," (speech, Boston Ad Club Brand Symposium, January 27, 2004).

CHAPTER 4

1. Copernicus Marketing web site (www.copernicusmarketing.com).

2. Brown-Forman Corporation 2004 Annual Report.

3. Janet Adamy, "Behind a Food Giant's Success: An Unlikely Soy-Milk Alliance," *The Wall Street Journal*, February 1, 2005.

CHAPTER 5

1. Edward Jay Epstein, *The Diamond Invention* (Arrow-Random House, 1982).

2. See www.forevermark.com for additional information.

3. Stuart Elliott, "MasterCard Revamps Print Ads," *The New York Times*, August 11, 2004.

4. The approval in late 2004 for American Express to issue cards through banks could dramatically change market dynamics and marketing strategies.

5. The American Legacy Foundation was born in 1998 as a result of the Master Settlement Agreement between 46 states and the major tobacco companies. The foundation's goal is to build a world where young people reject tobacco and where anyone can quit.

CHAPTER 6

1. Point of Purchase Advertising International web site, "The Retail Marketing Industry" (www.popai.com/AM/Template.cfm?Section=Industry).

2. Paco Underhill, *Why We Buy* (Simon & Schuster, 2000).

3. Deborah Ball, "Consumer-Goods Firms Duel for Shelf Space," *The Wall Street Journal*, October 22, 2004.

4. Tiffany & Company web site (www.tiffany.com/about/timeline.asp?).

5. John Beystehner (speech, Chief Sales Executive Forum, October 27, 2003).

6. The Advertising Century Report, *Advertising Age*, 1999.

7. Richard W. Lewis, *ABSOLUT Book: The ABSOLUT Vodka Advertising Story* (Journey Editions, 1996).

8. Target Corporation Annual Report, 2003.

9. Ibid.

10. Landor Associates and Penn, Schoen, and Berland, "Presidential ImagePower Study," August 6–11, 2004.

CHAPTER 7

1. Jim Edwards, "The Tracker: P&G Placements Triple Amid Cutbacks In TV Ad Spending," *Brandweek*, June 27, 2005.

2. Jordan S. Berman, "Branded Entertainment Workshop" (speech, iMedia Brand Summit, September 2004).

3. eMarketer web site, "New Interest in Branded Entertainment," March 30, 2005 (www.emarketer.com).

4. "Too much of a good thing?" *Brandweek*, August 9, 2004.

5. Stuart Elliott, "Greatest Hits of Product Placement," *The New York Times*, February 28, 2005.

6. Katherine S. Stone, "What Is Experiential Marketing?" Weblog posting (decentmarketing.typepad.com).

7. Consumer responses were gathered by Sponsorship Research International on October 20–22, 2003, via an online survey of 800 consumers in the United States, equally divided by gender and age (18–23, 24–37, 38–49, and 50–65). Data from Jack Morton Worldwide.

8. Stephanie Kang, "Mattel Creates a Living Barbie to Revive Sales," *The Wall Street Journal*, June 22, 2005.

9. David Kiley, "A New Kind of Car Chase," *BusinessWeek*, May 15, 2005.

10. Gina Piccalo, "The pitch that you won't see coming," *Los Angeles Times*, October 19, 2004.

CHAPTER 8

1. eMarketer web site, "Internet users in select countries...", May 1, 2005 (www.emarketer.com).

2. NOP World web site, "Influentials" (www.nopworld.com/products.asp?go=product&key=53).

3. *Forbes.com*, "Day in the Life of C-Level Executives, Part V," September 2004 (www.forbes.com).

4. David Verklin, "Crackle of Change" (speech, Boston Ad Club Symposium, March 9, 2005).

5. Pew Internet & American Life Project, March 2005.

6. Ian Beavis, "Mitsubishi Motors" (speech, iMedia Brand Summit, September 2003). Note: In May 2005, Mr. Beavis was named Vice President, Marketing, for KIA Motors America.

7. Kathleen Kerwin, "How Mercury Scored with Online Video," *BusinessWeek*, May 16, 2005.

8. iMediaConnection web site, "ING's Tom Lynch," January 23, 2003 (www.imediaconnection.com).

9. Ibid.

10. Ellis Booker, "Vonage Embraces Behavioral Targeting," *BtoB*, September 22, 2004.

11. David Verklin, "Crackle of Change" (speech, Boston Ad Club Symposium, March 9, 2005).

12. eMarketer web site, "New Interest in 'Branded Entertainment'" (report on a survey conducted by the Association of National Advertisers), March 30, 2005 (www.emarketer.com).

CHAPTER 9

1. Survey of 496 senior executives around the world conducted by the AESC, January 27, 2005–February 22, 2005 (AESC press release, April 19, 2005).

2. Rebecca Fannin, "Top 25 Brands," *Chief Executive*, November 2004.

3. Brent Schlender, "How Big Can Apple Get?", *FORTUNE*, February 21, 2005.

4. Ibid.

5. This and subsequent quotes are from Dan Hanrahan, interviewed by the authors, April 2005.

6. This and subsequent quotes are from Theresa McLaughlin, interviewed by the authors, February 2005.

7. This and subsequent quotes are from Larry Fish, interviewed by the authors, February 2005.

8. Sarah Ellison, "P&G Chief's Turnaround Recipe: Find Out What Women Want," *The Wall Street Journal*, June 1, 2005.

9. Robert Berner, "P&G: New and Improved," *BusinessWeek*, July 7, 2003.

10. Patricia Sellers, "Teaching an Old Dog New Tricks," *FORTUNE*, May 31, 2004.

11. Robert Berner, "P&G: New and Improved," *BusinessWeek*, July 7, 2003.

12. This and subsequent quotes are from Ron Lawner, interviewed by the authors, February 2005.

13. James Wynbrandt, *Flying High: How JetBlue Founder and CEO David Neeleman Beats the Competition...Even in the World's Most Turbulent Industry* (John Wiley & Sons, 2004).

14. The Editors, "The Most Powerful People in Golf," *Golf Digest*, October 2003.

15. Jack Kuykendall, "Moe Norman and the Titleist Deal," 2002 (www.scigolf.com).

CHAPTER 10

1. Fortune Brands 2003 Annual Report.

2. PGA.com web site (www.pga.com).

3. RTI/Legacy Media Tracking Survey, 2002.

4. Teen Research Unlimited Tracking Study, July 2001.

5. Matthew C. Farrelly, Kevin C. Davis, M. Lyndon Haviland, Peter Messeri, and Cheryl G. Healton, "Evidence of a Dose-Response Relationship Between 'truth' Antismoking Ads and Youth Smoking Prevalence," *American Journal of Public Health*, March 2005.

6. "iPod Sales Shine Up Apple's Profit," *The Wall Street Journal*, January 13, 2005.

7. Target Corporation 2004 Annual Report.

8. Louis V. Gerstner, *Who Says Elephants Can't Dance? Inside IBM's Historic Turnaround* (HarperBusiness, 2002).

CHAPTER 11

1. Special issue: "The Biggest Moments in the Last 75 Years of Advertising History," *Advertising Age*, March 28, 2005.

2. Research study by Accenture, according to Jessica Hodgson, "TiVo Technology Could Leave 10% of TV Ads Unwatched," *The Wall Street Journal*, June 23, 2005.

3. Michael McCarthy, "Vegas Goes Back to Naughty Roots," *USA TODAY* web site (www.usatoday.com).

4. Sandra O'Loughlin, "Hey, We're Number One!," *Brandweek*, June 27, 2005. America was proclaimed the number one brand among American consumers out of 2,400 brands measured by Young & Rubicam's BrandAsset Valuator.

Credits

All trademarks referenced in this book are the property of their respective holders.

CHAPTER 2

"The Top 25 Brands" courtesy of *Business Week*

CHAPTER 3

Figure 3-1: © Vatican Museum & Gallery/Bridgeman Art Library; courtesy of Royal Caribbean Cruise Lines and Arnold Worldwide

Figure 3-2: © Bill Cash; courtesy of Volkswagen of America and Arnold Worldwide

Figure 3-3: © Ibid, Inc.; courtesy of Citizens Bank and Arnold Worldwide

Figure 3-4: Courtesy of Citizens Bank and Arnold Worldwide

Figure 3-5: Courtesy of Arnold Worldwide

CHAPTER 4

Figure 4-1: Courtesy of Acushnet Company and Arnold Worldwide

Figure 4-2: © 2003 Jimmy Williams; all player images © Getty Images; courtesy of Acushnet Company and Arnold Worldwide

Figure 4-3: Courtesy of White Wave, a division of Dean Foods

CHAPTER 5

Figure 5-1: Courtesy of American Legacy Foundation and Arnold Worldwide

Figure 5-2: © Malcolm Venville; courtesy of Volkswagen of America and Arnold Worldwide

CHAPTER 6

Figure 6-1: Courtesy of White Wave, a division of Dean Foods

Figures 6-2 and 6-3: ABSOLUT ads used under permission by V&S Vin & Sprit AB (publ). ABSOLUT COUNTRY OF SWEDEN VODKA & LOGO, ABSOLUT, ABSOLUT BOTTLE DESIGN AND ABSOLUT CALLIGRAPHY ARE TRADEMARKS OWNED BY V&S VIN & SPRIT AB (publ). © 2005 V&S VIN & SPRIT AB (publ)

CHAPTER 7

Figure 7-1: Photo © Brian Garland; courtesy of Volkswagen of America and Arnold Worldwide

Figure 7-2: Courtesy of Royal Caribbean Cruise Lines and Arnold Worldwide

Figure 7-3: Courtesy of Tyson Foods and Arnold Worldwide

CHAPTER 8

Figure 8-1: Courtesy of Royal Caribbean Cruise Lines and Arnold Worldwide

Figure 8-2: Background photo © 2004 Michael Darter; courtesy of Royal Caribbean Cruise Lines and Arnold Worldwide

Figure 8-3: Courtesy of American Legacy Foundation and Arnold Worldwide

CHAPTER 9

"Top 25 Brand CEOs" courtesy of *Chief Executive* magazine

"Citizens Credo" courtesy of Citizens Bank

CHAPTER 10

Figures 10-01, 10-02, 10-03, 10-04: Created by Arnold Worldwide from market and company data sources

Index

About the Authors

Francis J. Kelly III is president and chief operating officer of Arnold Worldwide. He has worked with clients ranging from Jell-O and Johnson & Johnson to Titleist and Hewlett-Packard. Kelly has helped Arnold Worldwide to develop its Brand Truth creative philosophy and to grow into a nationally acclaimed agency, with clients such as Fidelity Investments, Jack Daniel's, Radio Shack, Royal Caribbean, and Volkswagen. Kelly holds an MBA from Harvard Business School and is coauthor of *What They Really Teach You at the Harvard Business School* (Warner Books, 1986).

Barry Silverstein, a senior vice president at Arnold Worldwide, has 30 years of experience in advertising and marketing communications. Before joining Arnold, he was CEO of his own direct and Internet marketing agency. Silverstein has worked with scores of leading clients, including Gillette, IBM, Sun Microsystems, Tyson, and Vonage. Silverstein is author of *Business-to-Business Internet Marketing* and *Internet Marketing for Information Technology Companies* (both from Maximum Press).